A SIGNIFICANT LIFE

TODD MAY

A Significant Life

Human Meaning in a Silent Universe

THE UNIVERSITY OF CHICAGO PRESS   *Chicago and London*

TODD MAY is Class of 1941 Memorial Professor of the
Humanities at Clemson University. He is the author of many
books, including *Friendship in an Age of Economics, Contemporary
Movements and the Thought of Jacques Rancière,* and *Death.*

The University of Chicago Press, Chicago 60637
The University of Chicago Press, Ltd., London
© 2015 by The University of Chicago
All rights reserved. Published 2015.
Printed in the United States of America

24 23 22 21 20 19 18 17 16 15   1 2 3 4 5

ISBN-13: 978-0-226-23567-7 (cloth)
ISBN-13: 978-0-226-23570-7 (e-book)
DOI: 10.7208/chicago/9780226235707.001.0001

Library of Congress Cataloging-in-Publication Data
May, Todd, 1955– author.
A significant life : human meaning
in a silent universe / Todd May.
pages cm
Includes bibliographical references and index.
ISBN 978-0-226-23567-7 (cloth : alk. paper) —
ISBN 978-0-226-23570-7 (e-book)
1. Philosophical anthropology. 2. Meaning (Philosophy)
3. Life. 4. Conduct of life. I. Title.
BD450.M335 2015
128—dc23
2014023736

♾ This paper meets the requirements of ANSI/NISO
Z39.48–1992 (Permanence of Paper).

CONTENTS

INTRODUCTION

I grew up in New York City, two blocks from the Museum of Natural History. I recall, many years ago, when the current Hall of African Peoples was constructed. The first time I entered it I was struck, for under the arch through which one enters the exhibit is inscribed the words "One is born, one dies, the land increases."

Those words haunted me then, and they haunt me still. Is it true that that's all there is? That we are nothing more than a long way around from loam to loam? Is there some reason for my being here except to live out my allotted time, to burn my days alongside others who are, in turn, burning theirs? It was that puzzle, that concern, that gnawing bewilderment, that led me along the path of literature and eventually philosophy.

We often ask ourselves questions like these when we think about our own death. There comes a time in the lives of most of us when the outlines of the far shore become more distinct than those of the shore from which we set out. We look backward and see life as a quarter over, half over, or nearly done. And we wonder, what have we made of ourselves? What have we been about? Whatever we have done to arrive at this moment, we have less time to alter it than we had to get here. We won't get a full do-over. Have we lived as we ought, or as we might? Have our lives been not just good, but meaningful?

Was there a point to them, or will there be? Or will we instead lie on our deathbed and say to ourselves, "It was the wrong life. I should have lived differently"?

After all, if there is a meaning to our living—or, if our lives are to be meaningful—then we don't have forever to find it. It is not as though that far coast will keep receding before us, allowing us a century or two to tinker at trifles here or there in the meantime. Indeed, we need to discover that meaning, or have it revealed to us, or perhaps even create it, in the limited and yet undetermined time that is our portion.

However, although death may motivate us to ask about the meaningfulness of life, it is not necessary for the question to arise. It can emerge in other ways, confronting us through other venues. The French philosopher Albert Camus writes of something similar which he calls a feeling of the absurd. "It happens that the stage sets collapse. Rising, streetcar, four hours in the office or the factory, meal, sleep, and Monday Tuesday Wednesday Thursday Friday and Saturday according to the same rhythm—this path is easily followed most of the time. But then one day the 'why' arises and everything begins in that weariness tinged with amazement."[1] Weariness tinged with amazement. The weight of the rhythm exhausts us, seems grinding where it once seemed natural, or didn't seem like anything, just background noise. At the same time we are perplexed by this rhythm, by the fact that we never noticed, or even that it was there at all. The fact of our being here, having gone through these motions for all these years without having noticed their pointlessness, grips us at the same time it bears down upon us.

For me, it first happened on the subway in New York. Coming home from high school, gazing over the faces of my fellow passengers, each staring into the middle distance; one day everything suddenly became futile. My life began to feel remote. The elderly Chinese lady across from me, nodding off every few seconds while trying to keep her shopping bags propped between her knees; the business man solemnly reading his folded copy of the *New York Times*; a teenager in jeans and a leather jacket trying to look intimidating: weren't we all just playing roles? As Shakespeare had it, we are all certainly just strutting and fretting our time upon the stage in a grand play. But who then is our audience and what, if anything, do our roles matter?

For Camus, these feelings of pointless rhythms or of death's inevitability are only the symptoms of the absurd. The absurd itself is something very precise. It is the confrontation of our need for meaning with the unwillingness of the universe to yield it to us. Humans need reasons; we need to know that there is some point to going on. The universe, however, is silent. It does not speak, or if it does, it is in a language we do not understand. It is not that there necessarily is no meaning. Perhaps there is. But if there is, it is inaccessible to us. Science might give us explanations. It might tell us why things are the way they are. But science does not yield meaning. That is not its job. And if we are to understand what the universe has on offer, where else could we turn?

Camus thought we have nowhere else to turn. We must live within the indifference of the universe, or better within the constant confrontation of our need for meaning with the universe's steadfast silence. It is a matter of remaining in this condition of dual refusal: our refusal to give up the quest for meaning and the universe's refusal to offer it to us.

Everything else, he thought, is a form of suicide. If we can no longer hold up our end of the bargain, abandoning our need for meaning, we can only do so through physical suicide. The human condition demands meaning; to eliminate the demand requires the elimination of our human condition. If we must have meaning in order to go on living, then we can't go on living. The feeling I had that day on the subway was not an illusion. There is no audience for my life that would give it a point. If I were overwhelmed by that, then I would be tempted by physical suicide. In fact, at moments I was.

The other form of suicide is philosophical. Instead of killing ourselves, we kill the thought that the universe will give us no reason to go on. Philosophical suicide is when we pretend that there is meaning to be found, and that it is enough to satisfy our longing. That pretense can take many forms. It can come in the form of a belief in God, or a reason that balks at its impotence and offers itself the illusion that it has found meaning. Or, in a more popular vein, it can come in the form of self-help books like *The Alchemist* or *The Secret*.

Either form of suicide, physical or philosophical, is a denial of the human condition. It is an act of cowardice in the face of our situation. The only integrity, for Camus, lies in facing it directly, in continuing to seek for meaning in a universe we already know will not offer it to us.

I always wondered about this. It is true that the daily rhythms of our lives and the inevitability of our death place the question of meaning before us. It is also true that the universe does not place any meaning of our lives before us. But, I asked myself, must this be all there is to the question of meaning? Human longing, a silent universe: did this exhaust the discussion? It all seemed too quick.

I decided that I must think more deeply, which in philosophy means more slowly, about what it is to seek meaning and about what might fulfill that search. I could not so hastily take the feeling of the absurd and ascribe it to the human condition, or take the silence of the universe as the last word on meaning. If I did, I would indeed wind up in the absurd. But if I must arrive there, I thought, let it be at the end of my reflection, not at the outset.

My hope is that at the end of this book, a way of thinking about what can make a life meaningful will emerge. It may not be the only way. It won't give us everything Camus wanted: a universe that yields to our reason. It won't give us anything grand. Meaningfulness, it turns out, might be more pedestrian than anything Camus sought. But if it won't give us everything, it will give us something. And perhaps, in the face of a silent universe, that will be enough.

Chapter One

A MEANINGFUL LIFE?

Let us start with a question. What does it mean to ask about the meaningfulness of life? It seems a simple question, but there are many ways to inflect it. We might ask, "What is the meaning of life?" Or we could ask it in the plural: "What are the meanings of life?" If we put the question either of these ways, we seem to be asking for a *something* or *somethings*, a *what* that gives a human life its meaningfulness. The universe is thought or hoped to contain something—a meaning—that is the point of our being alive. If the universe contains a meaning, then the task for us becomes one of discovery. It is built into the universe, part of its structure. In the image that some philosophers like to use, it is part of the "furniture" of the universe.

When we say that the meaning of life is independent of us—that is, independent of what any of us happens to believe about it—we do not need to believe that there would be a meaning to our lives even if none of us were around to live it. We only need to believe that whatever meaning there is to our lives, it is *not in any way up to us* what it is. What makes our lives meaningful, whether it arises at the same time as we do or not, does not arise as part of us.

The idea that something exists independent of us and that it is our task to discover it, is how Camus thought of the meaning of life. If our lives are to be meaningful, it can only be because the universe contains a meaning that we can discern. And it is the failure not only to have discerned it but to have any prospect of discerning it that causes him to despair. The silence of the universe, the silence that affronts human nature's need for meaning, is that of the universe regarding meaning itself.

The universe, after all, is not silent about everything. It has yielded numerous of its workings to our inquiry. In many ways, the universe seems loquacious, and perhaps increasingly so. There are scientists who believe that physics may be on the cusp of articulating a unified theory of the universe. This unified theory would give us a complete account of its structure. But nowhere in this theory is there glimpsed a meaning that would satisfy our need for one. This is because either such a meaning does not exist or, if it does, it eludes our ability to recognize it.

The idea that the universe is meaningful precisely because it contains a meaning independent of us is not foreign to the history of philosophy. It is also not foreign to our own more everyday way of thinking. It has a long history, a history as long as the history of philosophy itself, and indeed probably longer. One form this way of thinking has taken is that of the ancient philosopher Aristotle.

For my own part, I long detested Aristotle's thought, what little I knew of it. For me, Aristotle was just a set of sometimes disjointed writings that I somehow had to get through in order to pass my qualifying exams in graduate school. It wasn't until a number of years into my teaching career that a student persuaded me to read him again. In particular, he insisted, the *Nicomachean Ethics* would speak to me. I doubted this, but I respected the student, so one semester I decided to incorporate a large part of the *Ethics* into a course I was teaching on moral theory. Teaching a philosopher is often a way to develop sympathy for him or her. It forces one to take up the thinker's perspective. Before embarking on the course, I recalled the words of the great historian of science Thomas Kuhn, who once said that he came to realize that he did not understand a thinker until he could see the world through that thinker's eyes. In fact, he said that he realized this after reading Aristotle's *Physics*. I figured that if anything would do the trick with Aristotle, teaching his *Ethics* would be it.

It did the trick.

Not only do I find myself teaching the *Ethics* on a regular basis. Once, in a moment of hubris, I signed up to teach a senior-level seminar on Aristotle's general philosophy. In doing so, I told my students that I would try to defend every aspect of his thought, even the most obsolete aspects of his physics and biology. This forced me and the students to take his thought seriously as a synoptic vision of human life and the universe in which it unfolds.

Aristotle's ethics, his view of a human life as a trajectory arcing from birth to death and his attempt to comprehend what the trajectory of a good human life would be, has left its mark on my own view of meaningfulness. His attempt to bring together the various elements of a life—reason, desire, the need for food and shelter—into a coherent whole displays a wisdom rarely found even among the most enlightened minds in the history of philosophy. It stands out particularly against the background of more recent developments in philosophy, which often concern themselves less with wisdom and more with specialized problems and the interpretations of other thinkers.

Aristotle talks not in terms of meaning, but of the good. So the ethical question for Aristotle is, What is the good aimed at by human being? Or, to put it in more Aristotelean terms, What is the human telos? It is, in the Greek term, *eudaemonia*. *Eudaemonia* literally means "good" (*eu*) "spirit" (*daemon*). The term is commonly translated as "happiness." However, happiness as we use the word does not seem to capture much of what Aristotle portrays as a good human life. For Aristotle, *eudaemonia* is a way of living, a way of carrying out the trajectory of one's life. A more recent and perhaps better translation is "flourishing." Flourishing may seem a bit more technical than happiness, or perhaps a bit more dated, but that is one advantage it possesses. Rather than carrying our own assumptions into the reading of the term, it serves as a cipher. Its meaning can be determined by what Aristotle says about a good life rather than by what we already think about happiness.

Flourishing is the human telos. It is what being human is structured to aim at. Not all humans achieve a flourishing life. In fact, Aristotle thinks that a very flourishing life is rare. It is not difficult to see why. In order to flourish, one must have a reasonably strong mental and physical constitution, be nourished by the right conditions when one is young, be willing to cultivate one's virtue as one matures, and not face overwhelming tragedy during one's life. Many of us can attain to some degree of flourishing over the course of our lives, but a truly flourishing life: that is seldom achieved.

What is it to flourish, to trace a path in accordance with the good for human beings? The *Nicomachean Ethics* is a fairly long book. The English translation runs to several hundred pages. There are discussions of justice, friendship, desire, contemplation, politics, and the soul, all of which figure in detailing the aspects of flourishing. But Aristotle's general definition of the good for human beings is concise: "The human good turns out to be the soul's activity that expresses virtue."[2] The good life, the flourishing life, is an ongoing activity. And that activity expresses the character of the person living it, her virtue.

For Aristotle, the good life is not merely a state. One doesn't *arrive* at a good life. The telos of a human life is not an end result, where one becomes something and then spends the rest of one's life in that condition that one becomes. It is not like nirvana, an exiting of the trials of human existence into a state where they no longer disturb one's inner calm. It is, instead, active and engaged with the world. It is an ongoing *expression* of who one is. This does not mean that there is no inner peace. A person whose life is virtuous, Aristotle tells us, experiences more pleasure than a person whose life is not, and is unlikely to be undone by the tribulations of human existence. And a virtuous person, because he has more perspective, will certainly possess an inner calm that is not entirely foreign to the idea of nirvana. However, a good life is not simply the possession of that calm. It is one's very way of being in the world.

To be virtuous, to have any virtue to express, requires us to mold ourselves in a certain way. It requires us to fashion ourselves into virtuous people. Human beings are structured with the capacity to be virtuous. But most of us never get there. We are lazy, or we do not have the right models to follow, or else we do have the right models to follow but don't recognize them, or some combination of these failures and perhaps others. A human being, unless she is severely damaged by her genetic constitution or early profound trauma, can become virtuous, whether or not she really does. But to do so takes work, the kind of work that molds one's character into some-one whose behavior consistently expresses virtue. Most of us are only partly up to the task.

What is this virtue that a good life expresses? For Aristotle, virtues are in the plural. Moreover, they come in two types, corresponding to two aspects of the human soul. The human soul has three parts. There is the vegetative or nutritive part: the part that breathes, sleeps, keeps the organism running bio-logically. Then there is desire. It is directed toward the world, wanting to have or to do or to be certain things. But desire is not blind. It is responsive to reason, which is the third part of the soul. And because desire is responsive to reason, there are virtues associated with desire, just as there are virtues asso-ciated with reason. There are virtues of character and virtues of thought.

The vegetative or nutritive part of the soul cannot not have its own virtues, because it is immune to reason. Unlike desire, it cannot be controlled or directed or channeled. To be capable of virtue is to be capable of developing it. It is not to be already endowed with it. This requires that we can both recognize the virtue to be developed and develop ourselves in accordance with it. And to do that, we must be able to apply reason. I can apply reason to my desire to vent anger on my child when he has failed to recognize the need to share his toys with his little sister. In fact, I can do more than this. I can notice the anger when it begins to appear in inappropriate situations, reflect on its inappropriateness, lay the anger aside, and eventually mold myself into the kind of person who doesn't get angry when there is no need for it. With anger I can do this, but not with breathing.

The virtues of character include, among others, sincerity,

temperance, courage, good temper, and modesty. For Aristotle, all of these virtues are matters of finding the right mean between extremes. Good temper, for example, is the mean between spiritlessness and irascibility. It is the mean I try to develop when I learn to refrain from getting angry in situations that do not call for it, as with my child. If I never got angry at all, though, that would not display good character any more than a readiness to vent would. There are situations that call for anger: when my child is older and does something knowingly cruel to another, or when my country acts callously toward its most vulnerable citizens. Virtues of character are matters of balance. We reflect on our desires, asking which among them to develop and when. Sometimes we need to learn restraint; sometimes, alternatively, we need to elicit expression. We are all (almost all) born with the ability to do this. What we need are models to show us the way and a willingness to work on ourselves.

Virtues of thought, in contrast to virtues of character, are matters of reason alone: understanding, wisdom, and intelligence, for instance. The goal of virtues of thought is to come to understand ourselves and our world. Like the virtues of character, they are active. And like the development of virtues of character, the development of virtues of thought is not a means to an end. The goal of these virtues is not simply to gain knowledge. It is to remain engaged intellectually with the world. As Aristotle tells us, "Wisdom produces happiness [or flourishing], not in the way that medical science produces health but in the way that health produces health."[3]

This point is easy to miss in our world. In contrast to when I attended college, many of my students are encouraged to think of their time in a university as nothing more than job training. It is not that previous generations were not encouraged to think in these terms. But there were other terms as well, terms concerning what might, perhaps a bit quaintly, be called "the life of the mind." In 1998, the *New York Times* reported that "in the [annual UCLA] survey taken at the start of the fall semester, 74.9 percent of freshmen chose being well off as an essential goal and 40.8 percent chose developing a philosophy. In 1968, the numbers were reversed, with 40.8 percent selecting financial security and 82.5 percent citing the importance of developing a philosophy."[4] The threat faced at many universities to the humanities, from foreign languages to history to philosophy, signals a leery or even dismissive attitude toward a view of the university as helping students to "develop a philosophy." Aristotle insists that a good life is not one where our mental capacities are taken to be means to whatever ends are sought by our desires. It is instead a life in which our mental capacities are exercised as an end in itself. In fact, although we need not follow him this far, for Aristotle contemplation is the highest good that a life can achieve. It is the good he associates with the gods.

What might a good life look like, a life that Aristotle envisions as the good life for human beings? How might we picture it?

We need not think of someone with almost superhuman capacities. A good person is not someone larger than life. Even less should we think of someone entirely altruistic, who dedicates her life to the good of others. That is a more Christian conception of a good life. It is foreign to Aristotle's world, where a good life involves a dedication to self-cultivation. Last, we should not light upon famous people as examples of those who lead good lives. It may be that there are good lives among the famous. But a good life is not one that seeks fame, so whether a good person is famous or popular would be irrelevant to her. For this reason, we might expect *fewer* good lives among the famous, since public recognition often alights upon those who chase after it.

Instead, a good life is likely to be found among one's peers, but not among many of them. It would be among those who take up their lives seriously as a task, a task of a particular sort. They see themselves as material to be molded, even disciplined. Their discipline is dedicated to make them act and react in the proper ways to the conditions in which they find themselves. This discipline is not blind, however. It is not a military kind of discipline, where the goal is mindless conformity. It is a more reflective discipline, one where an understanding of the world and a desire to act well in it are combined to yield a person that we might call, in the contemporary sense of the word, wise.

It would be a mistake to picture the good life as overly reflective, though, and for two reasons. First, a good life, in keeping with the Greek ideal, requires sound mind and sound body. Cultivation of character is not inconsistent with cultivation of physical health. In fact, if recent studies are to be believed, good physical health contributes to a healthy mind. It is, of course, not the sole contributant. We cannot assume that because someone is athletic, he is a paragon of good character. On the contrary, the list of examples that would tell against this assumption would make for long and depressing reading. There is a mean to athleticism as there is a mean to the virtues. But the person lost to reflection, the person who mistakes himself for an ethereal substance or sees his body merely as an encumbrance to thought, is not leading a good human life. Even if, for Aristotle, contemplation is the highest good, it can only be sustained over a long period by the gods. The good human life is an embodied one.

Second, if a person cultivates herself rightly, then over time there should be less of a need for continued discipline. A good person will learn to act well automatically. It will become part of her nature. Someone who is flourishing, confronted with a choice between helping others where it would benefit herself and helping them in spite of the lack of benefit, would not even take the possibility of benefit as a relevant factor in the situation. It would remain in the background, never rising to the level of a consideration worth taking into account. The fact that she would benefit just wouldn't matter.

It is not surprising, then, that for Aristotle the person who does not think of acting poorly, for whom it is not even a possibility, is leading a better life than someone who is tempted to evil but struggles, even successfully, with herself to overcome it. The latter person has not cultivated herself in the right way. She may be strong in battle but she is weak in character. This is one of the reasons Aristotle says that a good life is more pleasurable to the one living it than a bad one. Someone who has become virtuous is at peace with herself. She knows who she is and what she must do and does not wrestle with herself to do it. Rather, she takes pleasure in not having to wrestle with herself.

It might be thought that the good life would be solitary or overly self-involved. But for Aristotle this is not so. In fact, what he calls *true* friendship is possible only among the virtuous. The weak will always want something from a friend: encouragement, support, entertainment, flattery, a sense of one's own significance. It is only when these needs are left behind that one can care for another for the sake of that other. True friendship and the companionship that comes with it are not the offspring of need; they are the progeny of strength. They arise when the question between friends is not what each can receive from the other but what each can offer.

The flourishing life depicted by Aristotle is certainly an attractive one. It is attractive both inside and out, to oneself and to others. To be in such control of one's life and to have such a sense of direction must be a rewarding experience to the person living it. As Aristotle says, it is the most pleasurable life. And from the other side, there is much good that such a life brings to others. This good is given freely, as an excess or overflow of one's own resources, rather than as an investment in future gain. It is a life that is lived well and does good.

But is it a meaningful life?

In order to answer that question, we must know something about what makes a life meaningful. If we were ask Aristotle whether this life is meaningful, he would undoubtedly answer yes. The reason for this returns us to the framework of his thought. Everything has its good, its telos. To live according to one's telos is to be who or what one should be. It is to find one's place in the universe. For Aristotle, in contrast to Camus, the universe is not silent. It is capable of telling us our role and place. Or better, since the universe does not actually tell it to us, whisper it in our ear as it were, it allows us to find it. What we need to do is reflect upon the universe and upon human beings, and to notice the important facts about our human nature and abilities. Once we know these, we can figure out what the universe intends for us. That is what the *Nicomachean Ethics* does. When Camus seeks in vain for meaningfulness, he is seeking precisely what Aristotle thinks is always there, inscribed in the nature of things, part of the furniture of the universe.

The problem for us is that we are not Aristotle, or one of his contemporaries. We do not share the framework of his time. The universe is not ordered in such a way that everything has its telos. The cosmos is not for us as rational a place as he thought. Perhaps it can confer meaning on what we do. But even if it can, it will not be by means of allocating to everything its role in a judiciously organized whole.

Some readers may balk at this. After all, for those who are theologically inclined, at least in a monotheistic way, doesn't God play the same role as the cosmos does for Aristotle? Doesn't God grant meaning to lives? Isn't a theologically grounded universe one in which it is possible that one's living is not in vain?

Aristotle's thought is different. Recall that for him the gods can contemplate the universe, but they do not confer meaning upon it or upon us. The rationality of the universe—that rationality out of which the telos of things emerges—is not given to it by something outside its structure. It doesn't come from God. It comes from the inside. It is part of the rational structure itself. Everything in the universe, we might say, is lit up by its own meaning, or at least carries the wick within it.

For monotheistic thought, the universe requires God in order to have meaning. Without God, the universe would be destitute. God reaches out and lights up each of us, just as Michelangelo's painting of God and Adam in the Sistine portrays the creation. That is why so many religious people find it difficult to understand how atheists can make any sense of their lives. Without a deity to give the point of things, what would be the goal, or even the appeal, of continuing to live? Without God, what is the motivation for soldiering on?

But then, one might think, the problem is solved without Aristotle. For even if there is no rational order supporting the meaningfulness of our lives, even if they are not lit up from the inside, nevertheless God can stand in as the guarantor of meaning. We may not live in Aristotle's world, but we need not live in Camus's either. There is a third option: a deity that grants meaning from the outside.

This is the option embraced by many people, although probably not self-consciously. It seems to me that it is instead taken up more or less reflexively. Rather than people's saying to themselves something along the lines of "Where can I find meaning?" and then seeing that God provides the answer to that question, the belief in God puts the question to bed before it has a chance to throw one's life into disarray. There are others, to be sure, who feel their lives to be without significance until they find God. They lead a troubled existence that is only becalmed when they come to sense the presence of God in their lives. But probably most believers are not like this. If the question of meaning arises for them, it is later, after belief has been established. And then the answer is already there. "What makes your life meaningful?" "Why, God."

Whether taken up reflexively or after a more or less tortured search, the belief in God provides a sense of meaningfulness to many people. Perhaps, then, we can ratify at least some of what attracts us about Aristotle's portrait of a good life without having to endorse the frame within which he paints it. We can say instead that the elements we find attractive are not the product of a rational cosmic structure but of theological intent. What is more, we don't have to rely on Aristotle alone for the answer to the question of what makes a life meaningful. We can incorporate some of his elements into a later conception, whether Judaic, Christian, or Islamic. Or we can look to those later conceptions at the outset and discover how much they converge with Aristotle's thought afterward. Or, if we like, we can simply forget Aristotle.

If we could rely on God to provide meaning, we would have our question answered for us. The answer, in fact, would have arrived on the scene before we did. All we would have to do is take it up, live it, and pass it on to the next generation. But, unfortunately, things are not so simple. This way of thinking about what makes life meaningful faces three challenges. Each challenge poses a different problem for approaching meaningfulness through God. And each is progressively more difficult to answer. This is because the first starts outside religion, the second from outside any particular religion, and the third from inside religion itself. The challenges are progressively more intimate, and therefore progressively more disturbing to those among us who rely on God, reflexively or not, to bear the burden of our meaning.

The first challenge is the most obvious. It is the challenge to belief itself. Its most popular contemporary representatives in the English-speaking world are Richard Dawkins, Daniel Dennett, Sam Harris, and Christopher Hitchens, sometimes ironically referred to as the "Four Horsemen." The latter two focus on what they perceive as the evil consequences of religious thought and practice: bigotry, divisiveness, violence. Dawkins and Dennett are more concerned with the scientific, and in particular evolutionary, case against the existence of God. If the moral case against the existence of God rests upon the idea that faith cannot ground decent living, the evolutionary case rests instead upon the idea that there is no need to appeal to God to explain who we are and how we got here. The former case is interesting in its own right, but it does not touch upon the question of whether God offers us meaning. It could be, for instance, that institutional religion is just a warping of God's message. If institutional religion promotes hatred and intolerance, that need not be God's fault. It could be the fault of those who speak in God's name or claim to be God's representatives. The task, then, would not be that of turning away from God, but of getting the message right.

It is the latter case—the evolutionary one—that concerns us here, since it returns us to Camus's silence of the universe.

The evolutionary case against religion is probably familiar to most readers. It is grounded in Darwin's idea that human life is not the result of conscious design but rather of historical happenstance. The reason there are human beings is not that anything (or Anything) intended it. It is instead that, in the unfolding of the natural world, one of the species that emerged and was able to reproduce under recent environmental conditions is ours. We were not anticipated by the universe, and our coming was not welcomed by it. Moreover, as we emerged, so we will disappear. Eventually, conditions will change in ways that will render us unable to pass on our genes and sustain the species population. In fact, if we keep living as we have been, inducing climate change and depleting the natural resources that nourish us, we are likely to cause our own disappearance. And if we do, that might, from some point of view, be ironic. But it would not violate the cosmic order. As a species we will have been born, we will have died, and the land will have increased.

One might ask here whether the evolutionary case against God's existence tells against a meaningful life. Might we look at how we have come down through evolutionary history and ask, for creatures like ourselves, what might make a life meaningful? It would be like asking Aristotle's question, only this time centered on biology instead of the cosmos. For science, though, that would be a stretch. If we're being biological about it, we might ask whether certain things make humans flourish in terms of our health or our psychological well-being, but to ask about meaningfulness is a different question, one that lies outside the realm of biology and other sciences.

In any event, the challenge presented by the evolutionary argument to the belief in God is a formidable one. We cannot, of course, resolve it here. That is not our task. But let us suppose that we could resolve it, and resolve it in favor of theological commitment. Let us suppose that there were reasons to believe in the existence of a deity or deities. Would that give us the grounding we need in order to recognize our lives as being meaningful or at least potentially meaningful?

Unfortunately, no. To grant the existence of God (or gods) does not allow us to grasp the meaning our lives might have. It does not trace out a path to meaningfulness. This is not because there is no path, or no roadmap. It is because there are too many. Once we grant the existence of God, or of a group of gods, then the question arises: which God and which roadmap? And without knowing which God or which gods deserve our belief, and which way that God or those gods have asked us to live, we don't know what meaning is the sanctioned one.

This difficulty is familiar to us. It has bearing on our concerns here because different religious traditions give different answers to the question of a good or meaningful life. We need not reflect upon the difference between monotheistic and polytheistic religions to convince ourselves of this. To be sure, the distinction between a Buddhist life of emotional disengagement and a Jewish life of Talmudic study or an Islamic life of prayer, almsgiving, fasting, and pilgrimage are real enough. But we need not cast our net so far in order to catch different, and perhaps contradictory, prescriptions for meaningful lives. In fact, we need even not appeal to different monotheistic religions. The problem emerges *within* monotheistic religious traditions. We can recall, for instance, the Protestant/ Catholic debate over faith versus works as the proper path for a Christian life. Is a truly Christian life fundamentally internal and private? Is it a matter of faith and one's personal relationship to God? Or is it, as Catholicism holds, a matter of the work one does, the good one produces in the world, and how one comports oneself with others? This debate goes to the heart of what makes a life meaningful within the context of a religious tradition. And its resolution, as the anguished history of Christianity displays, is not easily achieved. Given the elusiveness of the sacred texts involved in the debate, it is not clear that it can ever be achieved.

Were this a matter of science, the position we find ourselves in would not be so vexed. We might have difficulty in discovering what makes life meaningful, but we would at least have a common method of discovery. Through the scientific method, we could at least eliminate some possibilities while allowing others to remain candidates. The commonality of approach would allow us to recognize our differences and offer us more than a glimmer of hope that we might resolve them. (Perhaps this is why, although there have been fierce debates in modern science, there have been no wars.) But faith does not offer the sturdy ground of method to rely on. Different texts cannot be tested for adequacy, and the ambiguity of those texts leaves open competing and irreconcilable interpretations.

We need to be clear here, because philosophy, like religion, does not have a method as strict as the scientific method to rely on. Instead, it relies on reasons. Philosophy asks us to go where the best reasons take us. How far that is remains a complex question. What we are pointing to here is not a problem of the failure of reasons. It is rather this: that the determination of a meaningful life from a religious perspective requires one to choose a specific religious orientation in order to get the prescription for meaningfulness. And this, in turn, seems to make meaningfulness depend upon one's individual choice. It does not turn on any reasons one might have for that choice, or at least any reasons that might compel others to make the same choice. I have faith, if I do, because of reasons that are personal to me, not because of reasons that I think you ought to share as well.

It was this, ultimately, which drove me away from religion and toward philosophy. I spent several years of my life, in late high school and early college, seeking to know whether I should believe in God or not. I read Tolstoy and Dostoyevsky and eventually took college courses in religion, asking myself not what religion was or how it worked but solely the question of whether I had reason to believe in God, or a god of some kind. I didn't want personal reasons: that belief would give me comfort or offer a sense of community or make my life feel more well ordered. I wanted to know whether there was a God because answering that question, I thought, would answer the question of whether life is meaningful. And for that, there had to be compelling reasons that had nothing to do with my own desires. In the end, I realized that approaching things this way would be futile. The relation to a god has to be personal, a matter of faith. And for me, it was philosophy, not faith, that was driving my quest.

What we have been looking for is a universe that is not silent, a universe that can allow us to discern what makes or can make our lives meaningful. The hope was that the turn to religion, by giving us a deity that infuses the universe and our place in it with meaning, would offer us an abode for that search to come to rest. What we have found instead is a realm in which it is we that are asked to decide what gives meaning to our lives. Faith turns out to be not so much the discovery of meaning as an announcement of it. And that announcement relies on us, not upon the universe. Moreover, it does not rely on us as a collective, but on each of us individually. Finally, the announcement is in an important way arbitrary. There is no compelling reason to choose one deity (and one interpretation of that deity's message) over another. The announcement is as ungrounded as it is personal.

Faced with these difficulties, let us allow ourselves another assumption. Let us assume not only that there is a God, as we did in the face of doubt about religion itself, but also that we know which God and which textual interpretation is the right one. Wouldn't it be that, *if* we could know this, we would have access to the meaningfulness of life? It's a big *if*, to be sure, but doesn't this *if* allow us to hold out hope that the theological direction toward which we have turned might, in the end, yield us the answers we seek?

Not even this will help us.

There is a dilemma here, one that is often cast in terms of the good rather than meaningfulness. It is a dilemma that ultimately throws us back on ourselves, makes us the arbiter of what is good or meaningful. Like all dilemmas, this one has two horns. The first horn is this: suppose what is good is only what God decides to be good. What is good would be, by definition, whatever God chooses as good. Then God could choose that slavery or rape would be good, and that would make it good. The good, rather than being something we could discover or argue about, would be hostage to God's will. If God's will turns out to be fickle or arbitrary or to go against our own view of the good, then so be it. The good itself would be fickle or arbitrary or offensive to us.

We can see this idea at work in meaningfulness. Suppose that whatever God decided is a meaningful life for human beings would, by that very decision become meaningful rather than holy. Then God could decide that it was meaningful for humans to stand in a corner for as much of their lives as possible, or torture people of other races, and this would make it meaningful. A recent, and more amusing example would be to imagine something like Douglas Adams's *Hitchhiker's Guide to the Galaxy*, where the point of all living beings on earth is simply to be part of a supercomputer designed by superior beings to deduce the Ultimate Question of Life, the Universe, and Everything. (Those who read the book will recall that the answer to the question had already been discovered: 42. But the question to which it is the answer was still unknown.) Would we really find our lives meaningful if we discovered that each of us was simply a part of a chip in a computer programmed to solve a problem posed by beings in some other part of the universe? And would it help at all to know that those beings were superior to us? Would it help to know that that being was God?

This seems a caricature of God, and it is. Our image of God is not of a being who acts arbitrarily, either in the name of meaning or of 42. The God many of us worship is not a God who would see us as mere playthings. Our conception of God has perfection as one of its characteristics. A perfect being would not treat its creatures this way. The God of the monotheistic tradition is in all accounts a good God, not an evil or capricious one.

But this only leads us to the other horn of the dilemma. If God is good, then God conforms to the good. God cannot ground the good because God answers to it. The good exists, separate from and irreducible to God. It is God who casts itself in the image of the good, not the other way around.[5]

What goes for the good must go for meaningfulness. Not just anything can be declared meaningful. There must be some criteria for what is to count as meaningful, and however God thinks about the meaningfulness of human lives, it must conform to those criteria. The criteria are distinct from God. The meaningfulness of our lives, if there is any, cannot merely be a product of God's pronouncements. There must be something about the universe independent of God that offers human lives a sense of meaningfulness and that God itself must answer to.

But this path, we have already seen, is barred to us. It is, in fact, precisely *because* it is barred to us that we turned to God in the first place. We followed Aristotle in asking about a good or meaningful life, but parted ways with him at the point where he assumes that the possibility of such a life is part of the rational structure of the universe. It was there that we asked whether God could fulfill the role that a rational universe does for Aristotle. Perhaps it would be God that could ground the meaningfulness of a life for those of us in the contemporary world, those for whom the character of the universe itself is not enough for such grounding. But now we find that we are thrown back to the first option, the one we had abandoned. It cannot be God that supports the meaningfulness of our lives, because God, if it exists, must answer to it.

We seem bereft. We cannot count, with Aristotle, on the rationality of the universe to give meaning to human life. Nor can we count on God to grant it to us in the face of a universe that is not rational—or at least not rational in a way that includes meaningfulness. Regarding the meaningfulness of our lives, the universe is, as Camus argues, silent. Even invoking a God that Camus rejects does not give us the meaning he sought. Is this our situation?

In Dostoyevsky's *The Brothers Karamazov*, the intellectual Ivan Karamazov suggests that if God does not exist, then everything is permitted. Might it be that even with God—at least God alone—everything is still permitted? And also pointless?

Let us recall our latest discussion. What is meaningful cannot be simply what God would declare meaningful. It cannot be reduced to whatever God (or gods) would decide. This seems to lead us to the idea that if human life is meaningful, it is because there is a meaning independent of God and of us that a human life can conform to. But let us pause a moment here. When we ask whether life is meaningful, must we assume, with Aristotle—and even Camus—that for it to be meaningful it must be written into the nature of things? Must we assume that something outside of our lives must act as their guarantor? Must the two options be: an independent source of meaning and no meaning at all? Is there no third possibility?

Perhaps, even in a silent universe, not all choosing is ungrounded. Maybe some choices are more meaningful than others, not because the universe ratifies them, but for some other reason. And maybe that reason, or those reasons, can come from us in some way or another without being entirely arbitrary. To be sure, they will not have the imprimatur of the cosmos. But they might not be capricious, or superficial, or merely whimsical for all that. They would not possess the iron stolidity a grounding in God or the rational structure of things would lend them; but they might not lack all heft.

After all, the picture of a flourishing human life that Aristotle paints for us is attractive. Perhaps, even in the absence of the kind of universal guarantee that he associates with it, we might still have reasons for finding it attractive. And perhaps there are other lives as well that might be attractive in different ways: for their steadfastness or their intensity or their subtlety or their spontaneity. And, finally, perhaps that attractiveness is more than passing fancy, but is grounded in something deeper, something that can be given articulate shape.

This wager will require us to think about the meaningfulness of our lives differently from how we often do. Previously I said that meaning is often thought of "a *something* or *somethings*, a *what* that gives a human life its meaningfulness." That is how Camus and Aristotle and much of the religious tradition have thought of human meaning. If we are to make headway, it is precisely this way of thinking that we must abandon. We must approach the question of meaning differently. Rather than meaning being a *something*, it can be a *someway*: a meaningful life would be a life lived in certain ways rather (or more) than others. Human lives might become meaningful in the adjectival or adverbial sense rather than possessing a meaning in the nominative one.

To place this wager requires two tasks. The first is to say what this meaningfulness might be. What is meaningfulness if it isn't a meaning? What values does it involve? How does it assess the possibilities of a human life and sort them out so that some come to seem worthwhile? The second task is to account for how this meaningfulness, if it isn't underwritten by the universe or God, might nevertheless have a grip on us. Why should we believe that a meaningfulness that we generate can answer the concerns that have brought us to this point?

One might hope here that a wager like this, if successful, would redeem human life in a larger way. It will not. My aims are more modest than that. If the perspective I defend here is compelling, it will not justify each of our lives writ large. It will not redeem each of us in the face of the cosmos. And it will not give a sense of meaningfulness for humanity as a whole. One might say that it is too late in the history of human development for these projects to seem viable. In fact, it has probably always been too late for that. Burnishing the lives of each of us, or of all of us collectively, glossing them in a patina of cosmic acknowledgment, is a task that has always been beyond us.

What I seek here is only to offer a way of looking at our lives that allows us the possibility of creating them in such a way that they become meaningful—meaningful in a sense of the term that is significant, if not from the point of view of the universe then not solely from the private point of view of each of us alone. What is pursued here is a way of nourishing our hope for meaning on something other than our solitary choices, if not the universe's approval. Or, to put it another way, I would like to develop a perspective within which to recognize ourselves and our lives so that between our living, our dying, and the increase of the land, something worthwhile will have a chance of taking place.

But first we must speak of happiness.

Chapter Two

IS HAPPINESS ENOUGH?

Happiness—the topic of happiness—is in the air. People are wondering about it: what it is, who has it, how to get it. There has been a veritable explosion of studies of happiness. We now have a World Database of happiness, a *Journal of Happiness Studies*, and a *World Happiness Report*. According to one survey, Denmark is the happiest country in the world, and has been for several years.[6] If we go a little further back, we might admire Bhutan for initiating in 1972 an index for gross national happiness to replace that of gross national product. The issue of happiness is all around us.

There are lessons being offered about happiness. We are told that what we think brings us happiness—material goods—often doesn't, and that what we often take for granted—personal relationships—usually does. Related to this, we are told that we are not very good at figuring out what makes us happy. We mistake short-term pleasure for happiness, and wrongly predict what will bring us to a happier state. If we want happiness—and who doesn't?—then, we are told, we need to become clear on where to find it and how to cultivate it in our lives.[7]

All of this concern with happiness assumes that it is centrally important that we become happy. Perhaps happiness is the most pressing concern of a human life. Perhaps, in fact, it is not meaningfulness but instead happiness that should be our focus. What we seem to want, above all, is for us and those we care about to be happy. The refrain of parents everywhere, including my wife and me, is that we don't care what our kids do as long as they are happy. Happiness often seems the proper end of a life. A life that achieves it can be at peace with itself; a life that does not has fallen short.

We might be tempted to think that this concern for happiness has always been with us. Maybe it is a feature of human existence to seek happiness, and our contemporaries are just approaching it more systematically and scientifically than previous generations. After all, as we saw earlier, one translation offered for Aristotle's concept of *eudaemonia* is "happiness." But this comparison is misleading. *Eudaemonia* is not a matter of how we feel about ourselves or our world. It is a way of being whose features are inscribed in the cosmos. To be happy or flourishing is nothing other than to be a proper human being. Granted, Aristotle thinks that *eudaemonia* brings us pleasure. But that is a side effect of living a fully human life. It is not the goal.

What we in the modern world call happiness and what Aristotle calls *eudaemonia* cannot be mapped onto each other. For us, happiness is something personal. It is subjective, in the sense that it is a matter of what belongs to us, of what our experience is like. For Aristotle, *eudaemonia* is objective, in the sense that it is a way of being that is the goal of *any* human life. Imagine Aristotle confronting me about some activity I was engaged in—say, playing fantasy baseball—and telling me that this is not a proper activity for a human. And imagine I told him, as we often hear (and sometimes say), "But it makes me happy." What would be his response? I can imagine two different ones. He might say that I do not understand what happiness is, that happiness has nothing to do with what I'm feeling. Or instead he might say that happiness as I conceive it is not the proper telos of a human life. Either way, there would be something in his view that feels foreign to many of us.

If we think that happiness has always been a human concern, then, we must be careful not to assume that people have always thought the same way about happiness as we do. But if we are currently so concerned with happiness—with our conception of happiness—why is this so? What is it about our situation that provokes such fascination with what happiness is and how to get hold of it?

We might be tempted to think that it is because there is so little of it about. After all, these are difficult times. As I write these lines, the US remains mired in an ongoing recession, and Europe cannot seem to escape the crisis of the euro. Greece, Italy, Spain, and Portugal are at risk of losing a generation of youth to unemployment. China's growth has slowed. People around the world are feeling insecure. This insecurity is economic, to be sure, but economic insecurity, particularly on such a vast scale, promotes unhappiness. It might be that in some cultures there can be poverty and happiness at the same time. But economic insecurity and happiness are rarely compatible.

The contemporary concern with happiness, however, seems to be of longer standing. It is not only since 2007 or 2008 that this outburst of concern with happiness has arisen. It can be traced back at least a decade or two. There is something in contemporary life that presses upon us, asking us to ask ourselves about our happiness. What this is, is difficult to say. There are some standard responses: the anonymity of individuals in mass society, the role of technology in isolating us from one another, the rise of an economic order that encourages us to treat ourselves and one another as capital rather than as human beings. There may be some merit to one or another of these responses, or to each of them in its proper degree. However, for our purposes there is a more urgent question than that of how our culture came to be focused upon happiness. It is whether happiness is the right focus in the first place. That we are preoccupied by happiness is undeniable. Ought we to be? More particularly, ought we to be preoccupied with happiness rather than meaningfulness? Should our journey veer from the path of meaning, turning instead toward the happiness that has assumed such popularity?

At an initial glance, happiness seems to be a more promising candidate for focusing on in thinking about our lives. We have already seen some of the difficulties in thinking about meaning. This alone might give us reason to abandon the quest in favor of happiness. After all, if neither God nor the cosmos is capable of offering us a conception of a meaningful life, much less a path toward one, how are we even to begin to approach our lives by way of meaning? Better a happiness we can understand than a meaningfulness whose nature and grounding remains a mystery.

There is more to say in favor of happiness. It isn't just that it is easier to understand than meaningfulness. We can say two more things in its favor at the outset. First, there is something very American about it. After all, doesn't the Declaration of Independence "hold these truths to be self-evident, that all men are created equal, that they are endowed by their Creator with certain unalienable Rights, that among these are Life, Liberty and the pursuit of Happiness"? What could be clearer than that? We might differ with one another—and with Aristotle—

about what happiness consists in. We might need to learn more about what makes us happy or how to pursue it. But that happiness and the right to its pursuit are deeply embedded in America's self-conception can hardly be doubted.

But there are those for whom such a consideration might not count for much. Not everyone, of course, is an American. And even among Americans, there are those who do not identify with this particular strain of American history and culture. However, a second consideration counts in favor of happiness, one that is related to American history but does not require aligning oneself with the view of the founding fathers. There is something democratic about focusing on happiness, especially when compared with meaning. If meaning is something objective, something out there independent of my life, it appears to be something that I must conform to—at least if my life is to be meaningful. If there is an objective meaningfulness, I could fail to achieve it even if everything else in my life is okay. It is as though I must reach beyond myself, beyond my life, my desires and hopes and even what I love, in order to fulfill the requirements of meaning.

Happiness is different. It is not about attaining a standard outside of me. Instead it concerns the character of my own life. It is personal. Happiness is about whether the trajectory of my days is unfolding in a way that is satisfying to me rather than whether it measures up to a standard outside of me. And this makes it more democratic. Each of us can decide whether we are happy or not. Each of us can pursue happiness in our own way and be the final arbiter of whether we have achieved it. This does not mean, of course, that we never need any assistance in being happy. We are likely to learn something from psychologists who experiment with happiness, or from reading the *Journal of Happiness Studies,* or from asking about why the Danes seem so happy. Happiness need not be pursued in isolation, divorced from the world and the insights of others. But if each of us is the final authority regarding his or her happiness, then happiness takes on a democratic character that goes missing with meaning.

This thought is American, but not only American. It is a thought that will be familiar to anyone in a society not in thrall to a traditional religious conception of a good life. In much of the world, people are no longer gripped by the idea that there is a single way to live and that everyone whose life is to be worthwhile must conform to that way. The loosening of this grip is captured by the word *tolerance.* For most of us, although we might not be attracted by ways of living very different from our own, we feel the need to tolerate those ways— at least up to a certain point. Even many people who are conservatively religious feel that others' approaches to living, although inferior in the eyes of God, are at least approaches to which they have a right. That each of us should be allowed to carve his or her own path through existence—assuming that path does not block the path of others—is a view deeply embedded in the modern world.

This view seems to be better accommodated by the idea of happiness than meaningfulness. It feels more natural to say that each person has a right to their own happiness than to say that each has a right to their own meaning. The latter rings false. There is something about meaning that detaches it from people's personal experience, which is why Aristotle thinks it is embedded in the cosmos and Camus, for his part, thinks it doesn't exist. It's not that we can't *say* that each of us can create their own meaning. We can say it. But what do we mean by it? Something like this: each of us decides what makes his or her life go well; each of us decides what is important and pursues it. When we recognize this, however, we can see that it is not really meaning in the sense discussed in the first chapter that we are talking about. It is not something that will give heft to our projects, nor is it something that will redeem the arc of our lives. It is instead something we declare without grounding it in anything other than that declaration. It's particular to us, to each of us. And that particular character is better captured by the idea of happiness than of meaningfulness.

Perhaps then we ought to jettison the search for meaningfulness and rest content with a search for happiness. Perhaps the idea of meaning is simply a relic of an earlier time, when people thought, with Aristotle or with the early monotheistic religious tradition, that human meaning was either part of the furniture of the universe or a gift from God. And maybe what puzzled Camus was not so much the silence of the universe as an idea—the idea of meaning—that he failed to recognize we have already outgrown. Perhaps we should substitute "the pursuit of Happiness" for the hankering after meaning, take on board the insights of recent happiness studies, and get on with our lives. After all, if we are to spend the limited time allotted to us seeking an illusion, bewitched by a concept that, upon reflection, no longer holds sway, then we are bound to be disappointed. We are fated to look back upon that search, and for all one knows upon our lives, with regret.

Before we commit to this path, before we allow meaningfulness to slip away from us and embrace happiness as a better framework for thinking about our lives, we ought at least to reflect a bit more on happiness. After all, up until this point

I've been throwing the term around pretty carelessly. I have been discussing happiness as though it were obvious what it meant. But, as we have seen, in philosophy to think more deeply is to think more slowly. It is time then to think a little more slowly about happiness. In particular, it is time to ask two questions. First, what is happiness? If we all have a right to pursue happiness, what is it that we have a right to? After all, even though what makes each of us happy is different, there must be something common about the happiness that these different things make for us. Otherwise we would not use the same term for all these distinct experiences.

Second, and this is the deeper problem, is happiness a more worthy pursuit than meaningfulness? If we cannot come up with an adequate view of what happiness is, then it won't serve us any better as a way to think about our lives than meaningfulness. It won't offer any criteria to tell us when we are happy or what we are seeking when we seek happiness. Imagine that you ask me what I should try to attain in life and I answer, "Happiness." In response, you ask what this happiness is that I should try to attain, and I have no answer to offer you. It won't help to tell you that whatever makes you happy will do. We have already acknowledged that one of the virtues of thinking in terms of happiness rather than meaningfulness is that it allows people to decide for themselves what makes them happy. It gives each of us the power to create a vision of a worthwhile life.

But that is not the issue. We are not interesting in what makes people happy, but in what happiness is. Without knowing this, *happiness* is just an empty word, a nonsense sound. It doesn't help us get on with our lives. To say that people should pursue what makes them happy would have no more sense than saying that they should pursue "whatever." And that is not very helpful in trying to get a grasp of how to construct one's life.

There is another reason for asking what happiness is. It returns us to the second question I asked a moment ago. It is only when we know what happiness is that we can ask whether it is worth pursuing in the first place. I suggested that happiness seems initially to be a better candidate than meaningfulness as a way to frame thinking about our lives. This is because there is something more democratic (and, for some, something American) about doing so. And this in turn is because our understanding of happiness is of something more personal than meaningfulness. What makes us happy depends on each of us rather than upon some outside criterion. But all of this is only an initial impression. It may or may not be justified by thinking about happiness more slowly. In order to see whether happiness really does work as an adequate framework for thinking about our lives, we need to investigate happiness further.

The first task in that investigation will be to ask what happiness is. Once we know that, then we will be in a position to assess its adequacy.

Our situation is a bit tricky here. Eventually, we will want to know whether happiness offers a better framework for thinking about our lives than meaningfulness. But at this point, we don't really have a good definition of either one. It would seem then, that even if we had a definition of happiness we couldn't compare them. We would be comparing something we understand with something we don't. How could we possibly do that?

Things are not as dire as they seem. There is another path

to take. We can ask what happiness is, and then ask whether it gives us what we want. Does a happy life, as we define happiness, meet the longings we have to live in a worthwhile way? Does it answer to the concerns that motivated the reflections of the previous chapter? If it does, then our journey will have ended. We will have arrived at our destination. If it does not, then we can ask why it doesn't. We can ask what it is about happiness that falls short as a way to frame reflection on how to go about our lives. And then we can ask whether there is a way of thinking about meaningfulness that can give us what is lacking in happiness.

This second path is a longer one, and more winding. But it must be our path. We have already seen traditional accounts of meaning fail in one way or another to answer to the aspiration to live a meaningful life. They do not address the haunting fear that there is nothing more to our days than being born, dying, and the land increasing. In following the path that offers a chance to avoid this fate we are unlikely to trace a direct route. If that were possible, it would probably already have been done. I could report the results, or refer you to the proper place to look. But I cannot do that, because there is no place to look.

What is happiness? We can begin with a simple answer. The answer can be traced back to the English philosopher Jeremy Bentham (1748–1832), who argues that what is most important to do in this world is to create the most happiness. Happiness, he tells us, is pleasure. It is pleasure because pleasure is what humans seek. In the opening lines of his most famous book, *An Introduction to the Principles of Morals and Legislation*, Bentham tells us, "Nature has placed mankind under the governance of two sovereign masters, *pain* and *pleasure*. It is for them alone to point out what we ought to do, as well as to determine what we shall do. On the one hand the standard of right and wrong, on the other the chain of causes and effects, are fastened to their throne. They govern us in all we do, in all we say, in all we think."

We seek pleasure and avoid pain. And because of this, our happiness lies in pleasure. There is something attractive about this idea. For a start, it is simple. It gathers our diverse experiences of happiness under a single concept, one that we can relate to. I know when I'm experiencing pleasure and when I'm experiencing pain. They are not hidden from me. I can imagine someone saying to me that my life is a meaningful one even though I don't know it. I can imagine someone saying to me that my life is a morally good one even though I don't recognize it. But I can't imagine someone saying to me that I'm experiencing pleasure but I don't know it. Pleasure is hard to miss. It may be that when I'm feeling just a little bit of pleasure it escapes my attention. It is never hard to discover, though, when it's happening. All I need to do is turn my attention toward my present experience to make it available to me.

We all know what this is like. "Wow, this is great." "I like this." "Yeah, I guess I'm having a good time." These are those moments of turning, those moments when we recognize what we are experiencing and it meets our approval. They are the moments when we notice the pleasure that has accompanied us, kindling our engagement with the world.

And what worthwhile experiences *don't* seem to be accompanied by pleasure? Pleasure attaches itself to so many of them. There are, of course, the obvious ones: eating good food, sex, a massage, being on the winning side of just about anything, receiving a gesture of approval from someone one respects, falling asleep after a tiring day. But there are others as well, ones that might not ordinarily be taken to involve pleasure. For many years, before my knees had their say, I was a runner. I ran every morning with a group of very good runners. One of them was—and as I write this, still is—among the best runners of his age group in the country. Running, as a sport, is not usually associated with pleasure. In fact, it is the ability to sustain pain that often tells who will prevail in a longer race. I can remember one race, my best one as an older runner, where I took the initial part of the race at too fast a pace. I had been running well, and got a little overconfident. I ran the first mile in a time that, given my ability, I was simply not entitled to. About two miles into the 5K (3.1 mile) course, I started to flag. My stomach began churning, lactic acid filled my muscles, my eyesight went dim. The course was a twisting one, so I told myself to make it just to the next turn, and then to the next one, and then the next one, until I saw and then sprinted to the finish line.

Where was the pleasure in that? I could have watched a college football game instead (the race was on a Saturday afternoon) and avoided all that pain. But I would never have had the pleasure I experienced knowing that I fought my way to my best time. That pleasure was not only different from relaxing in front of the television. It was far greater. In fact, as I write these lines I still feel a tingling of pleasure recalling the moments after the race when I reflected on what I had done.

We all have moments like that, moments when pain undergone yields to a pleasure that redeems it, a pleasure that could not have been had without suffering the pain first. For some of us, it happens after we complete a project that we have spent time and energy on: finishing a design for a new building or car or even an improved corporate flow sheet, or constructing a tree house for the neighborhood kids, or turning the last page of James Joyce's *Ulysses* after weeks of struggle. For others, it shadows more quiet pursuits: writing in a journal, playing a videogame, even sitting on the back porch at night pondering the stars. For still others, it partners with adventure or danger. Although I am deathly frightened of heights, I imagine rock climbers to be infused with an adrenaline rush as they hang suspended above a ravine or a river.

Perhaps, then, if we define happiness as pleasure, we have our object. We can say with Jeremy Bentham that people pursue happiness, that happiness is pleasure, and that therefore our lives consist in the pursuit of pleasure. We can let go of the more vexed question of meaning and commit ourselves instead to pleasure as a more fruitful framework for thinking about how to go about living. This would not satisfy Aristotle, nor would it impress Camus, but maybe this is because they are after something that should no longer concern us. In our world especially, with access to such a variety of goods through travel, the Internet, shopping, and television, we should take a view like Bentham's and make it ours. (To be sure, many people in our world don't have access to these goods; but then we should say that the problem is that they ought to have access, because that is what will make them happy.)

If we follow Bentham, we will have certainly answered the first question: what is happiness? At least, we will have given *an* answer. But we must still face the second question: is happiness—defined as pleasure—worth pursuing? Or, to be more precise, is it a framework within which we should structure how we think and act in regard to our lives? Will pleasure calm the concerns that we raised in the first chapter? No one doubts that pleasure is good. A life devoid of any pleasure at all would certainly be missing an important element of human flourishing. It would likely be a sad thing. And, as we have seen, pleasure is encrusted in many of our activities—or at least in their outcomes. But is pleasure enough?

There are some famous experiments in psychology that focus on the "pleasure center" in the brains of rats. In these experiments, an electrode is implanted in a rat's brain where the pleasure center is thought to exist. The electrode is connected to a bar that the rat can press. Then the rat is placed in front of three bars. If it presses one bar, it gets access to water. A second bar gives it access to food. A third bar is the one connected to the electrode. If the rat presses that one, it gets a jolt of pleasure. What do rats do in this situation? You have probably already guessed. They neglect the water and food and keep pressing the bar that gives pleasure. They do so until they cannot lift their paws to the bar any more. They often die. But they die happy.

My understanding of these matters—and, granted, it is a very limited one—is that things are more complicated for human beings. I am told that human pleasure isn't located in a single part of the brain. Instead it is a complex combination of chemicals and brain areas. But no matter. Let us imagine we could build a pleasure machine for human beings. (Some people think we already have: the television or the Internet.) The pleasure machine would be as complicated as it needs to be in order to give the maximum pleasure humans can experience. Here is one way it could work. There would be a set of electrodes implanted in the right places in the brain that would set off the chemicals and stimulate the brain areas that produce pleasure. To make sure there aren't any loose wires hanging from one's head, we can imagine that the electrodes could be activated wirelessly. This machine would then perform the same function in humans that the electrodes do in the experiments on rats.

Now suppose that you were offered this possibility. You could have the electrodes implanted in your brain. They would be subject to continuous stimulation. You would be given food and water, so you wouldn't starve. You would get adequate sleep. So you would live a life of complete pleasure. You would have pleasure at every moment. Also, because you would be sustained through proper nourishment, you would live to a ripe old age. But here's the catch. You wouldn't be able to do anything except sit there and be stimulated by the pleasure machine. You would experience continuous pleasure, but you wouldn't be able to *do* anything.

Would you take the offer?

I wouldn't. I have hardly ever met anybody who would. From time to time I bring up this example in my philosophy classes. Almost none of my students have ever said, "Where do I sign up?" (Every once in a while someone expresses interest.) There seems something awful about such a life, even if it is enjoyable. But what is awful about it? After all, it does meet Bentham's view that people pursue pleasure. In fact, according to his criterion, a life of continuous electronically stimulated pleasure might be the best life for a human being. Why do so many of us balk at it?

Such a life isn't really living. It is missing much of what makes a life worthwhile: relationships with others, challenges to overcome, goals to be achieved, activities to be immersed in. We might call all these things, for lack of a better term, life projects. An existence of continuously experienced but passively received pleasure doesn't have any life projects. When we ask what we would like of our living, almost all of us think of our family and friends, our work or our outside hobbies, the plans we have for the future, as central to it. A life without projects would be less than a life, or at least less than a life any of us is likely to choose.

This reveals something about the examples of pleasure I cited a moment ago: racing, designing a building or a car or a flow sheet, building a tree house, reading *Ulysses*. It is the projects themselves that call to us. The projects are not simply means to the pleasure we might get when we finish them. If they were, we would welcome the pleasure machine, since it cuts out the middle man of the project and leaves us with only the pleasure. But we don't welcome the pleasure machine. This is because it is not simply pleasure that makes our lives worth living. Or, to put it another way, pleasure doesn't answer to the longing for meaning we discussed in the first chapter. If we are to put that longing to rest, we cannot do it by substituting pleasure for meaningfulness.

Does this mean that we have to abandon happiness as a framework for thinking about our lives and return to the question of meaning? That would be too quick. We haven't shown that happiness cannot substitute for the longings we associate with seeking a meaningful life. The pleasure machine doesn't teach us that. All it teaches us is that if we think of happiness in terms of amounts of pleasure, then we cannot quell those longings. Maybe, then, we should think of happiness, or even pleasure, differently. Many philosophers have done so. One of the best is John Stuart Mill.

Mill thinks that Bentham is on to something with his discussion of pleasure, but that he approaches it too crudely. The problem, in his view, is not with thinking of happiness in terms of pleasure, but with thinking of it in terms of *simple* pleasure. For Bentham, pleasure is only a matter of the more and the less. For Mill, there are not only different amounts of pleasure; there are also different kinds of pleasure. Specifically, there are higher and lower pleasures. Not only is more pleasure preferable to less, but higher pleasures are preferable to lower ones. And, in fact, higher pleasures that yield lower amounts of pleasure are often preferable to lower pleasures that yield greater amounts of pleasure.

But how are we to tell which among our pleasures are the higher ones and which are the lower ones? Mill offers a simple test. Between two pleasures, the higher one is the one preferred by those who have experienced them both. He tells us, "Of two pleasures, if there be one to which all or almost all who have experience of both give a decided preference, irrespective of any feeling of moral obligation to prefer it, that is the more desirable pleasure."[8]

Like most people, I like to fritter time away. I enjoy that feeling of avoidance, particularly when I know that I'll have time to complete whatever tasks are awaiting me by their assigned deadlines. Whiling away moments, or even hours, in idle chat or trawling the Internet or walking around campus or sipping on a latte gives me a recognizable pleasure. But so do the projects I'm avoiding. Writing, teaching, learning a language: these projects offer their own pleasure. To be sure, they are often difficult (especially language-learning, which seems to be an activity for which my brain has not been wired). When I am doing them, though, they capture my attention. I become immersed. Moreover, if I were asked whether I would prefer the pleasure of one of these projects or that of frittering time, I would not hesitate to choose the former. Squandering stray moments has its gratifications, but I would undoubtedly select writing and teaching and (yes, even) learning French or Spanish over idleness if forced into a decision between them.

Is Happiness Enough?

This is Mill's point. For some reason, he presses it a bit further, arguing that, among all the pleasures that could be experienced, philosophy is at the pinnacle. In a famous passage, he writes, "It is better to be a human being dissatisfied than a pig satisfied; better to be Socrates dissatisfied than a fool satisfied. And if the fool, or the pig, are of a different opinion, it is because they only know their side of the question."[9] We need not follow him this far. His point remains that we don't think of pleasure simply as a matter of quantity. Pleasure is not only about the more and the less; it is about the better and the worse, or the higher and the lower. And Mill has given us a way to distinguish the two.

One might want to quibble with Mill here about his method. After all, is it clear that everyone, or almost everyone, would choose the same pleasures as the higher ones, and the same pleasures as lower? Mill himself, in claiming philosophy as the highest pleasure, has certainly plumped for a controversial choice. I could line up dozens of current and former students of mine who, having experienced philosophy, would beg to differ. They would be willing to offer any number of other activities as preferable to pondering questions of meaning, value, and existence. And to complicate matters, they would likely disagree among themselves about which among the other activities were better. There seems no reason to expect convergence on the distinction between higher and lower pleasures.

I don't think this quibbling would have bothered Mill. He could respond that even if the distinction between higher and lower differs among individuals, this does nothing to undermine his approach. There doesn't have to be universal agreement on which pleasures fall into each category. We only have to agree that people who experience various pleasures will be able to rank them as higher or lower. If people can do that, then they are not captive to a picture of pleasure like Bentham's that can only classify it in terms of amounts. That, in turn, means that happiness is a more nuanced concept than Bentham thought, and we need no longer be concerned about the problem of the pleasure machine. The pleasure machine can offer us more or less pleasure. It cannot offer us higher or lower pleasures.

Suppose we could redesign the pleasure machine. Suppose that, instead of offering us pleasure, the machine offered us experiences. The philosopher Robert Nozick, who thought it up, calls it the "experience machine."[10] How would such a redesign look? It would have to be more complicated than the pleasure machine. We could imagine it working this way. Whatever experiences one wants to have can be typed into the machine. If someone wants to have the experience of writing a novel, he simply has to type it in. Or if someone wants to experience what it is like to try to swim the English Channel, she can enter it into the machine. In each case, that is the experience they will have. The machine creates a virtual reality for its user, like that headgear one can don in order to have the visual experience of alternative worlds. The only difference is that the virtual reality created by the machine is not only visual. It is a complete experience. While immersed in it, one does not even know that it is only an experience. It would feel real.

However, it would not be real. It would only be an experience of what it would be like to do something that one is not actually doing.

The question about this new machine is the same as for the pleasure machine. If you were offered it, would you take it? If you had a choice between on the one hand living your life as you do now, taking your chances on the future, and on the other hand having the guarantee of whatever virtual experiences you like in the machine, would you trade in the real for the virtual? You could, of course, make the experiences as challenging as you like. You could make them as intimate as you like. You would get all the pain and all the pleasure associated with those experiences. In fact, you would believe you were having them, until the experience was over. And if you liked, you could type in a single experience—say a romantic love— that would last you a lifetime, so that from the moment you typed it in until you died you would feel that sense of being in love. Would you quit your own life for this one?

I can't imagine for a moment that I would take that deal. The experience machine is no more tempting than the pleasure machine. It might be neat to try for a couple of hours, but so might the pleasure machine. To look upon a lifetime of unreal experience is a repulsive prospect. While it might not seem like torture if I were already in it, it certainly seems so now. And, as with the pleasure machine, hardly anyone I've asked has ever been drawn to it.

Why is this? What is the difference between a life we would want to embrace and the lives offered to us by the pleasure and experience machines? If we long for a life worth living, a life that we have called one of meaning, what is lacking in these machines that we would ask of our lives? Neither of these lives, the life of pleasure or of virtual experience, is real in the right way. Of course, they are real in the sense that we would be really living in them—if there really were pleasure and experience machines. But they aren't real in another, more vital, sense. They aren't engaged with the world. They are solitary experiences that don't bring us in contact with others, with things, with activities. They aren't projects. Or better, they aren't *our* projects. They are only fantasy projects.

If happiness is going to put our longing to rest, then we

need to be able to think of happiness in a more sophisticated way. We need an account of happiness that gets us in touch with the world. This is tricky, because the idea of happiness is subjective; that is, it has to do with how we are relating to the world. The problem with Bentham's and Mill's views of happiness is that they made happiness *too* subjective. In their views, our relation to our environment gets lost. The gears of our lives don't mesh with those of the world. What is needed, perhaps, if happiness is to fulfill the aspiration toward a life worth living, is a take on happiness that focuses not only upon the feeling of happiness but also upon the engagement that gives rise to that feeling. It isn't just in what we feel, but in what we're feeling it about, that happiness consists.

Recently, a book has been written that answers precisely to this need. The philosopher Daniel Haybron's *The Pursuit of Unhappiness* is an account, based on both philosophy and psychology, of happiness as a type of engagement with the world. The reason for the book's title is given in its subtitle: *The Elusive Psychology of Well-Being*. Haybron argues that we are often mistaken about what makes us happy. In order not to be mistaken about it, we need to understand correctly what happiness is.

Happiness, rather than being an experience or a passing feeling, is an emotional relation to how one's life is going. It is deeper than experiences or feelings, deeper and more sustained. Being happy is "an individual's responding favorably, in emotional terms, to her life—responding emotionally to her life *as if* things are generally going well for her."[11] Rather than residing in pleasure or experience, happiness is a relation. It is a particular alliance between oneself and one's life, an alliance that he calls "psychic affirmation."

This alliance has three layers: attunement, engagement,

and endorsement. Attunement is the foundational layer. It happens when the world appears as a secure rather than hostile place. To be attuned is to be at home in one's life. It is difficult to be attuned when the world seems to be bearing down: when the job is stressful, the marriage is vexed, a close friend is very depressed, the mortgage payment isn't being met, the kids are a source of worry. The inverses of all these—a rewarding job, halcyon marriage, flourishing friends, stable kids—allow one to navigate the world more serenely and confidently. Attunement is not itself happiness, but it is hard to imagine being happy without the sense that one can steer confidently through one's days.

Engagement is built upon attunement. Haybron uses the term *flow* to describe it, a term he borrows from Mihaly Csikszentmihalyi,[12] as in "being in the flow." To be engaged is to be consumed by the task at hand, to be absorbed by it. When one is in the flow, self-consciousness melts away, energy levels rise, and one becomes lost in activity. There is a slang term, often used in sports, for this flow. People say a player who is in the flow is *unconscious*. The former hockey player Wayne Gretzky described it well. He said that there were times on the ice when he didn't see other players. Instead, he saw patterns. He could see how the patterns were unfolding and how they were going to look a few seconds later. So he would simply send the puck where it needed to be when the pattern changed. The puck would arrive at the stick of a fellow player or would sail past others into the goal. At those moments, there was no awareness that he was Wayne Gretzky or that he was playing hockey. There was only the pattern calling to his stick.

It is often difficult to be engaged without being attuned. Insecurity makes people self-conscious. It throws them back on their vulnerability. Lacking assurance in our actions, it becomes impossible to get into the flow of activity. Alternatively, having confidence allows us to abandon ourselves to our projects. The world opens up, and we jump in.

The final layer is endorsement. This is the layer most often associated with happiness, and the layer closest to the idea of pleasure. To endorse one's engagement is to affirm it. It is to say—or at least to feel—a yes to the life that is being led. Endorsement is the felt contentment with things as they are. It often involves a sense of success, if not in the outcome, at least in the process. While engagement is being in the grip of an activity, endorsement is the sense that that activity is going well. It is not merely evolving; it is blossoming.

Endorsement that is built on attunement and engagement does not suffer the problems we have seen with pleasure. To be sure, endorsement is pleasurable. It is the place that pleasure appears in this view of happiness. But this pleasure is not disconnected from living. To the contrary, it is founded on it. I would not be able to endorse my life in Haybron's sense from within the pleasure or experience machine. There would be nothing for me to endorse, since there is nothing I am engaged with that offers itself up for endorsement. I might be able to say yes to what was happening to me. But that's not what Haybron means by endorsement. Endorsement concerns who I am and what I am doing. It does not concern what I am feeling divorced from the life that I am leading.

The layered relation to one's life of attunement, engagement, and endorsement is what Haybron calls psychic affirmation. "Actually to be happy is for one's emotional condition to embody a stance of *psychic affirmation* in response to one's life: emotionally responding to it as to a favorable life—a life that is broadly going well for one, with only minor problems at most."[13]

Is Happiness Enough?

This picture is an attractive one. Happiness as Haybron describes it seems to bring us closer to what we seek in a worthwhile life. It is difficult to imagine a life that we would want to live that did not have something very close to what Haybron describes as happiness. I'm sure there are some lives without such happiness that have their attractiveness: lives of great accomplishment accompanied by self-doubt, or altruistic lives where sacrifice for others is seen as both necessary and difficult. But for most of us, a life without any attunement, engagement, and endorsement would be impoverished.

Such a life cannot be had in an experience machine. It would have to be lived. This does not mean that it would have to be lived intensely. Haybron recognizes this. "Perhaps some people can flourish by simply *being there*."[14] But even simply to be there is to be in one's life in a particular way. It is to be there in the real world, not in a virtual one.

Happiness may be a crucial element of a worthwhile life. But is it enough? Would a happy life offer us what we would have sought from a meaningful one?

Imagine yourself near the end of your life. You're confined to your bed. It is evening. Your loved ones, who are here to visit you in your last days, have left the room to order dinner. You look out the window, see the dusk settling over the trees, and look back upon the course your living has taken, the choices you made and the ones you left aside. You consider the shape of your life. Was it worthwhile? Was it a life you would have wanted to live? None of us, except the very charmed, gets *the* life we would have wanted to live. But was it *a* life worth having lived? Did it amount to anything?

And suppose you considered this for an answer: You were happy. It was a life you felt more or less secure in, one where you were able to focus on and feel good about what you did. You were a manager in a large company, or a doctor, or a carpenter, and you were absorbed by your work. You had satisfying relationships with your friends, your partner or partners, your children. Perhaps, like me, you ran competitively in your free time; or perhaps instead you played chess or went for walks or bowled or read novels in coffeehouses. In all of these things, you felt involved while you were doing them. Your days passed without your noticing them, without their passage intruding on you, because you were engrossed in your life.

You were happy. Would that be enough?

If happiness were the best you could manage as an answer to the question of whether your life was worthwhile, would you not feel that you had missed something? Would you not wonder whether there should have been something more to it than that? There is something about happiness that feels to many of us, in a particular way, too subjective. I don't mean that it feels too self-absorbed. Most of us have our happiness enriched by involving ourselves with others, and by doing things for them. Happy lives are generally not self-absorbed at all. Happiness seems too subjective in a deeper way. I can put it like this: it feels as though there must be more to a life than just *my being happy in it,* even in the rich sense of happiness that Haybron describes. It is that *more* that motivates the longings we described in the last chapter: the *more* that seeks God or a universe that answers to our desire for meaning.

In some of my darker moments I have pictured the world as being entirely bereft of that *more,* but without self-absorption. It is a picture in which we assist one another so that none of us is suffering, all of us living as well as we can, but all of us recognizing that ultimately this living is pointless. It may be better that we help one another than that we don't, and better that we live well rather than badly, but in the end we all know that we are born and we die and the land increases. Our mutual assistance is tragic: we do it, and in some way perhaps it is good of us to do it, but the shadow of futility hangs over all of us.

What is this shadow if not meaninglessness?

If happiness is not enough, it is because we feel the need to have our lives ratified from some perspective that isn't just that of our own happiness. When we wonder about a meaningful life, it is precisely that perspective that we are asking about. It is something outside of me that lends my life significance that I am asking after. Something outside of me, but to which I have access. Happiness, because it is not outside of me, cannot answer to it. But if the universe cannot and God cannot provide the answer, and if happiness cannot substitute for it, then where can I find it? Is it our human fate to remain bereft of significance, condemned at best to a rootless happiness?

For much of my life, this is how the matter stood. I had read the existentialists in college, and had come to believe with them that life is without any meaning other than what we impose upon it. This seemed the last word on the matter, and eventually I became content to live with it. But then, several years ago, I read a book that opened up a new path for thinking about the meaningfulness of life. That book, the philosopher Susan Wolf's *Meaning in Life and Why It Matters*, does not answer the question of meaning. It does not say, "Here's what the meaning of a human life is." What it does instead is open up a new way of thinking about meaningfulness. It allowed me to approach the question of meaning from a different angle.

Some books of philosophy have the effect on me of saying things that, once said, seem so obvious that I wonder why nobody had ever thought of that before—or why I had never thought of it. Wolf's book is one of those. Her central thought, although the product of deep reflection, is remarkably simple. She sums it up in a single phrase: "Meaning arises when subjective attraction meets objective attractiveness."[15] And she expands the idea this way: "A person's life can be meaningful only if she cares fairly deeply about some thing or things, only if she is gripped, excited, interested, engaged. . . . One must be able to be in some sort of relationship with the valuable object of one's attention—to create it, protect it, promote it, honor it, generally to actively affirm it in some way or other."[16]

Meaningfulness, she contends, is two-sided. There is a subjective side, the side of my own experience. If my life is to be meaningful, then I must somehow be involved in it, absorbed by it. The words Wolf uses to describe this absorption—gripped, excited, interested, engaged—may remind you of Haybron's discussion of happiness. I believe they should. Haybron's account of happiness is very close to what Wolf means by subjective attraction. For a human life to be meaningful, it must be one in which I am not a spectator but a real participant, and a participant in something that matters to me. That something can be any number of engagements: relationships, social change, work, athletics, or some combination of these. I have previously used the word *projects* to refer to them. For my life to be meaningful, those projects have to feel like *my* projects: not in the sense that I own them, but more in the sense that they own me, that they have captured my focus.

Why is this subjective side important? Why shouldn't we say that a person could live meaningfully even if they weren't happy in that life, if it didn't absorb their interest? Surely there are many good people who have contributed to the world and all the while being depressed or self-doubting or emotionally remote. What makes their lives less meaningful than those who feel involved in their projects?

It is important to distinguish a meaningful life from a good one. A person can live a perfectly good life—one that contributes to society or is loyal to friends and family or accomplishes an important feat—without feeling absorbed by what he or she does. There are people who sacrifice their own well-being for the sake of others, and we admire them. They are good people. Their lives certainly do not have less value than those who do the same thing but without its feeling like sacrifice. The latter may feel better about their lives, but they are not better people.

But to be a good person who has lived a good life is not the same as having a meaningful life. Wolf would like to reserve the word *meaningful* for lives characterized by a sense of engagement. People who feel alienated from their lives, however good they might be, lack something important, something that lends a richness above and beyond whatever decency their goodness displays. We already have a term for people who contribute to the world or to others. We call them good. Meaning, in Wolf's hands, is reserved for a life that might involve goodness, but is more than that. As she tells us, "If one usually finds her daily activities boring, if she typically feels alienated from the roles and projects she is nonetheless bound to occupy and pursue, if she is inclined to describe herself as feeling empty or even dead inside as she goes through the motions of her life, then that life is less than satisfactorily meaningful."[17]

The subjective side is only half of it. What I am gripped by, engaged in, must be a *valuable object*. It must have *objective at-*

tractiveness. This is the other half. Happiness is not enough.[18] We hope for our lives to amount to something more than being personally fulfilling. We seek to understand ourselves in terms that refer not only to our experience but also to some standard outside of that experience. We want our lives to measure up. This is what Wolf is calling our attention to by appealing to the adjectives *valuable* and *objective.*

Wolf asks us to imagine someone whose life is centered on caring for her goldfish. There is, of course, nothing wrong with having goldfish. And, as with all pets, it is good to ensure that their living conditions are favorable. With goldfish, I suppose, one should make sure that they have enough food, clean water to swim around in, and a plastic plant or two to vary the environment. It's also probably fun for goldfish owners periodically to relax in front of the goldfish bowl and let themselves be hypnotized by the repetitive motion of the fish's swimming back and forth. What Wolf asks us to picture is someone with much more invested in her goldfish than that. She asks us to imagine "a woman whose world revolves around her love for her pet goldfish."[19]

Let us imagine this. This woman, call her Mary, has feelings for her goldfish that many of us would reserve for our children or maybe our closest friends. When she awakens in the morning she immediately checks to make sure the goldfish is okay. She thinks about it when she is at work and hopes it has not run into any problems. If, one day or another, the goldfish seems sluggish, she is consumed with worry. She sits by its bowl monitoring its movements, wondering what she can do to make it feel better. We can even envision Mary talking to her goldfish, recounting her day, sharing her resentment of a colleague, confessing her struggle with her weight.

Because Mary's life is oriented around her goldfish she is

not involved in activities that many of us would find fulfilling. Her human relationships are superficial. She is not a part of her community. She doesn't have any other hobbies—or at least any that would interfere with her ability to care for her goldfish. The goldfish is the center of her life.

It is possible, although a bit strange, to imagine that Mary is happy. Assuming that her goldfish is thriving in its bowl, she feels peaceful and confident in her world. She is certainly engaged with her goldfish and is content with her engagement. She recognizes that she is unusual in this way, but thinks there is nothing wrong with her life. There are many people the world considers odd. She is just one more.

What are we to say of Mary? Some might call her pathetic. Others might feel a bit sorry for her, but think that if that's what makes her happy, then there's nothing wrong with it. Wolf would say that her exclusive commitment lacks the objective attractiveness necessary for her life to be meaningful. Or better, since meaningful can be a matter of the more and the less, that her life is not *very* meaningful. After all, caring for another living being counts for something. But an obsessive engagement with a living being that requires only minimal care and that won't benefit from human love is low on the scale of objective attractiveness. Because of this, Mary's life is a barely meaningful one.

To say that her life is hardly meaningful, however, is not to say that it is worthless. We need to keep in mind what Wolf is on about. She is not offering standards for judging the value of a life. She is offering standards for judging its meaningfulness. There is no reason to conclude from a lack of meaning that there is a lack of any kind of value. Mary's life is, in some sense, perfectly fine as it is. The world would experience a loss if she were suddenly to die. However, on the proposal that Wolf has put before us, her life's activities are not very objectively attractive, and so not very meaningful.

We can see this clearly if we shift our focus from humans like Mary to nonhuman animals, especially those that aren't pets and have no young to care for. Most animals without offspring spend their time foraging for food, sleeping, and warding off danger. There is little in this that we would be tempted to call objectively attractive. Their activities don't add much to the world. But that doesn't mean that they themselves are without value. Their very existence has a significance that is worthy of some sort of respect. Perhaps they don't deserve the same level of respect that humans do. Nevertheless, it would be callous to say that they are beneath all regard.

The lives of these animals are not very meaningful in Wolf's sense. Yet they are not worthless. The same is true of Mary.

There are some who may balk at saying that a meaningful life must be objectively attractive. In the course of thinking about these issues, I have occasionally discussed the example of Mary and her goldfish with others. Often, I am confronted with the same response. Why, I am asked, is Mary's life not very meaningful? Who am I to make the judgment that her life lacks (much) meaning? If it is fulfilling to her, if *she* is not seeking something more than her relationship with her goldfish, then how can someone who is not in her shoes make a judgment about the meaningfulness of her life?

It does not always settle their doubts when I distinguish meaningfulness from other kinds of value. There are those who balk at the analogy with nonhuman animals. They are quick to point out, rightfully so, that most nonhuman animals cannot think about their lives in sophisticated ways.

They can't decide that they would rather live in one way or another. Humans can. Mary can. Since she, unlike many animals, has chosen the path she has taken, what reason is there to say that her life lacks something important, something like meaning, that other human lives possess?

As it turns out, there is a reason for saying this. The problem with allowing just anything to be meaningful, without standards or criteria, is that it does not address the need for meaning we recognized in the previous chapter. Most of us want to live a meaningful life. We want there to be some point to our years. To say that any way of living will do as long as we are happy is not so much to answer that concern as to abandon it. It is to walk away from the difficulty.

To be sure, facing this difficulty has its own costs. One of them is that we might not discover anything that answers to our question. We might wind up in Camus's position. Another one—and this is the worry people have brought up to me—is that if we discover a standard of meaningfulness, some people, maybe ourselves and maybe others, will not measure up. In our own case, that would be distressing. In the case of others, it seems overly judgmental.

If what we seek is meaningfulness, and not just happiness, this is a cost that must be paid. It cannot be avoided. To have a standard of any kind entails the possibility that there will be times when the standard is not met. It does not matter what the standard is. It can be admissions criteria for college, a moral duty, a qualifying time for entering a race, behavioral or sartorial expectations for people who want to enter a particular social group or clique. Or it can be objective attractiveness for meaningfulness. To ask for a standard that will ground the meaningfulness of a life involves risking the possibility of realizing that one has fallen short, or that others have.

The other side to this coin, however, is a more hopeful one. Standards give us goals. They point out a direction for us, so that we know where to go. To have a standard for meaningfulness not only implies that my life—or Mary's life—might not be very meaningful. It would tell me where to find meaningfulness, so that I can go about the business of making my life more meaningful. If I know where I am lacking, I also know what I need. And isn't that really what the longing for meaning desires? Not a ready-made justification for who one happens to be at the moment, but a guide for becoming someone whose life embodies or expresses a larger significance.

Without a standard of objective attractiveness, we simply don't have that guide. If all lives are equally meaningful, then aren't all lives equally meaningless? What would be the difference between this way of seeing things and Camus's view? We would remain bereft. As Wolf tells us, in words that would have made Camus sigh in agreement, "Humans have a tendency to aspire to see things, including themselves, without bias, to observe their lives from a detached perspective. They aspire to a kind of objectivity."[20]

We need to have a standard of objective attractiveness if we are to address our longing for meaning. We must discover some way of thinking about what makes a life meaningful that does not appeal to the structure of the universe or to God, but that isn't merely inside our own skin. Where are we to find it?

At this point, we must take leave of Susan Wolf. She recognizes the importance of the question, but has no answer for it. "To the question, 'Who's to say which projects are independently valuable and which are not?' my answer is, 'No one in particular.' Neither I, nor any group of professional ethicists or academicians—nor, for that matter, any other group I can think of—have any special expertise that makes their judgment particularly reliable."[21] Wolf worries, as she should, that there is a danger of elitism in seeking to profess what the standards for objective attractiveness are. She is concerned that if she or anyone else were to take the reins on this problem the result would be an arbitrary declaration rather than a real answer.

Nevertheless, she does make judgments about certain lives that assume that there must be some kind of answer. She appraises the life of the goldfish caretaker that we have called Mary, or a person who spends her life smoking pot or doing crossword puzzles, and finds them wanting. Alternatively, she refers to sitting by the hospital bed of a friend or making a Halloween costume as examples of meaning. These examples resonate for many of us, which suggests that we at least have a *sense* of what makes a life meaningful. But she does not translate that sense into a standard.

For our part, we cannot leave matters there. If we are to reflect on our lives, to ask whether they are meaningful in such a way as to open the possibility of an answer, we must take up the task of developing criteria for meaningfulness. If happiness is not enough, if we seek meaning beyond the borders of our skin, and if we cannot rely on the universe or a God to give it to us, then we must confront the question of standards. We must be able to offer ourselves an answer to the question of what makes a life meaningful aside from its being endorsed by the person living it. Otherwise, Camus would be justified in asking us why we think our lives more meaningful than that of Mary or the pot smoker or the animal who cannot reflect upon its life.

In confronting this daunting task, we can take solace in this: we need not develop *the* conception of objective attractiveness. We only need to develop *a* conception. There may be others. It is possible that, aside from any standards we might discover or develop, there are ways of judging the objective attractiveness of a life that we have not considered. That would be fine.

In fact, it would be more than fine. It would allow us to allay Wolf's worry about elitism. If we can determine a way of thinking about what makes life meaningful that offers genuine criteria against which to assess our lives while not claiming that they are the only criteria, then we steer between the Scylla of meaninglessness that haunts Camus and the Charybdis of elitism that troubles Wolf.

It is an attractive prospect. But the prospect of an answer is not an answer. The challenge is to make good on the prospect. Where can we look to discover objective criteria of what makes life meaningful that does not rely on the universe or on God? In what light can we consider our lives in order to have emerge for us a way of seeing them as meaningful, or potentially meaningful? How can we think about ourselves, turn ourselves at a new angle, recognize ourselves differently, in order to discover something that might be objectively attractive about our lives?

Chapter Three

NARRATIVE VALUES

Our lives unfold over time. We are not just heaps of moments, each one piled on the others like grains of sand. Instead, we have trajectories. We arc from past to future. In this we are different from many other animals. Their horizons extend from the near past to the near future. To be sure, many of them have a sense of themselves. They fear death and do what they can to avoid it. But they do not recognize themselves in a biographical way. We humans do, however. Our past belongs to us, and our future extends before us as ours.

William Faulkner once wrote through one of his characters, "The past is never dead. It's not even past." We live our past, not only as past but as part of who we always are. Faulkner's point here is easy to miss. It is not just that the past causes us to act in certain ways. The past does do this, but that is not his point. The past is not just causally related to who we are; it *is* who we are. We are who we were, and who we will be.

This does not mean we cannot change. Of course we change. We can become so altered that we hardly recognize what we were once like. But even that change is us. We are who we were and who we are now as well as the change that has transformed us from one to the other. That stretch, that sweep, from who we were to who we are to who we will be: that is our life. The question we are asking—about whether lives can be meaningful—is about that stretch. It is a question about the thickness of time through which our living happens. To ask whether a life is meaningful is not to ask whether it is meaningful at this or that moment. It is to ask whether the whole (or at least the whole up to that point) is meaningful. Is that trajectory which is my life a meaningful one, or does it lack all significance?

We have seen that, if we seek meaning in our lives, we cannot make due with happiness. It is not that happiness is unimportant. A life destitute of happiness would be a difficult existence. But happiness cannot substitute for meaningfulness. It will not give us what we are after in asking about meaning. We need something more *objective*, in the sense we gave to that term in the last chapter. We require criteria to which we might live up, above and beyond our own fluid engagement with the world. We don't need the final word on meaning. There may be other criteria that will do as well. But we do need something.

A fruitful place to start is with the recognition that human lives are trajectories, unfolding over time. If we were creatures solely of the moment, meaningfulness—if we could locate it—would look very different from what it might look like for temporal beings like us. For us, to want a life to be meaningful is to want that life, in its entirety (or at least much of its course) to be redeemed by the criteria we use to assess it. It is a life, not its isolated moments, which is the subject of our reflection.

This recognition is not a novel one. It is, of course, Aristotle who first called my attention to it. "The happy [i.e., flourishing] person has the [stability] we are looking for and keeps the character he has throughout his life . . . he will neither be easily shaken from his happiness nor shaken by just any misfortunes. He will be shaken from it, though, by many serious misfortunes, and from these a return to happiness will take a long and complete length of time that includes great and fine successes."[22] For Aristotle, a flourishing life is developed and sustained over time. The flourishing person is not someone who happens to act well in one situation, and then in another one, and then again in a third, as though each were unconnected from the others. Instead, humans must take the resources they are given, develop them into a flourishing life, and then sustain (or, in cases of great misfortune, restore) that flourishing over the course of their personal histories. Acting well is one of the ways a flourishing life expresses itself; it is not, however, the very substance of flourishing. It is instead an *expression* of flourishing.

To ask about meaningfulness, we can take up Aristotle's cue. What, we might ask, makes a life trajectory meaningful? What gives proper shape to its course through time?

If we see ourselves this way, there is an approach that naturally suggests itself. We can call it a narrative approach. Since human lives unfold over time, perhaps what gives them meaning is their narrativity. Lives can be conceived as stories, with beginnings, middles, and ends. And like stories, lives can be seen as having plots, themes, major and minor characters, and perhaps even leitmotifs.

When we get to know someone, a friend or a lover, sooner or later we want to know their story. It is a way of getting to know who they are. I have a friend here at my university whom we hired into our philosophy and religion department five or six years ago. He and I have become close over those half dozen years. At first, my interest in him was simply professional. We wanted a good young philosopher, and he seemed to fill the bill. As is often the case, we occasionally had lunch together and talked shop. But incidental references to other activities in his life made him seem more interesting than just a good colleague would be. He had once sported a Mohawk. He had personal knowledge of several of the impoverished Baltimore neighborhoods detailed in the television series *The Wire*. He had gone out with a poet, and is married to a painter. Plus, he has a penchant for the ironic comment that, sometimes uncomfortably, captures the spirit of the moment.

I became curious. Who is this person who, when I first met him while we were interviewing people for the job, appeared only as a promising young scholar? What tied him to these other nonphilosophical aspects of his life? Why had he once had a Mohawk, and why does he not have one now? Through what course—and it is never a straight path—had he become interested in the odd field of philosophy? In short, what was his story?

Over the run of the past several years, some of these questions have been answered for me. And as they have been answered I have felt that I have come to understand, to a certain extent at least, who my friend is. A narrative of his life has taken shape for me, and that narrative seems to answer to my curiosity about him. This is not to say that I know everything about him. Nor is it to say that he is reducible to the plot of his life that I can now recount. Rather, in coming to possess a narrative account of his life, I feel that I have developed a sense of who he is.

What goes for others in this way seems also to go for ourselves. As we reveal ourselves to others, as we want others to get to know us, don't we often do so by means of narratives of our own lives? In telling others who we are, don't we usually tell stories about ourselves? To be sure, we do more than tell stories. We say what books or movies we like, how we react emotionally to one situation or another, which colleagues we respect and which we find insufferable. But these facts about us are themselves tied to our stories. Our preferences, our emotions, whom we respect: all of these have narratives behind them that tell them how we came, for instance, to be someone who likes *The English Patient* but not *The Corrections*, has a passion for ponderous European films, or takes pleasure in long-distance running.

And in sharing our stories with others, don't we occasionally come to see ourselves in new ways? I can recall, for instance, telling my wife about my vexed relationship with my father, one where I never really felt him to be genuinely impressed by anything I had done. (This is a cliché, I know, but only because so many people live it.) Later, when I expressed my frustration with my boss at the time for not recognizing my accomplishments, my wife helpfully recalled how similar this was to my earlier relationship with my father. This helped me both understand and get out from under my feelings about my boss. This part of the narrative of my life, awakened for me by my wife, allowed me to understand my current situation and how I was reacting to it in a fresh way. It was no longer just a question of the boss's failings, but also of my own reaction to people like him.

There is, in fact, a recent movement in psychotherapy that is deeply tied to stories. It is called narrative therapy, developed largely by the recently deceased therapist Michael White. In rough terms, narrative therapy says that who we are is largely a product of the stories we tell ourselves about who we are. If our stories have themes of things never working out, we become people for whom things don't work out. If our stories have themes of fear, we become fearful. In other words, our narratives about ourselves don't merely reflect who we are: they help produce who we are.

This doesn't mean that there are no facts to which our stories respond. It is not a matter of making things up—or at least not mostly so. Our stories concern the way in which those facts fit together. They create the plot and the themes that we think our lives consist in. And in creating these, we become complicit in the creation of our lives. We come to live the stories we think we are living.

As narrative therapy recognizes, some of the stories people tell themselves are disempowering. They recount lives in a way that makes it difficult to see a way forward. The therapeutic practice, then, is to investigate with people who feel disempowered different and more empowering stories they might tell themselves. Like the more disempowering stories, these other narratives need to respond to the facts of a person's life. But they weave those facts together in a different way, revealing other sides of people and allowing them to become engaged with their world in a more satisfying way. We might say that, in creating new narratives, people *reproduce* themselves into what they would rather be.

The idea that we live narratively is not restricted to narrative therapy. Recently, the role of stories in the shaping of our lives has become the focus of a number of philosophical and psychological views of who we are.[23] The prominent psychologist Jerome Bruner tells us "that it is through narrative that we create ourselves, that self is a product of our telling and not some essence to be delved for in the recesses of subjectivity."[24]

Perhaps, then, if we seek to understand how our lives can be meaningful, we should look toward their narrative character.

We should reflect on the stories that people tell themselves about their lives, to see whether we can glean something meaningful in those stories. This would capture the temporal character of human life—its trajectory or its sweep. We need not worry about whether we are discovering *the* meaning of life. Our task is not one of isolating everything that might make a life meaningful. It is enough if we could find *something* that offers meaningfulness. And for that, looking at the narrative character of human lives might provide a clue.

In approaching meaningfulness through narrative, there are two difficulties we will need to face. The first is that not everyone lives narratively. Some of us, when we reflect on our lives, see them in terms of stories. Perhaps we don't see them as single stories. They may be stories with multiple layers, or even multiple stories. But others do not see a narrative arc to their lives. Recently, the philosopher Galen Strawson, in an article provocatively titled "Against Narrativity," argued that there is no necessity to conceive a human life in narrative terms. Strawson contrasts what he calls "Diachronic" self-experience, in which one thinks of oneself narratively, with what he calls "Episodic" self-experience, in which "one does not figure oneself, considered as a self, a something that was there in the (further) past and will be there in the (further) future."[25] And he argues that there seems no reason not to consider an Episodic life as less worthy or less human than a Diachronic one. In fact, he finds himself to be "relatively Episodic . . . I have absolutely no sense of my life as a narrative with form, or indeed as a narrative without form. Absolutely none. Nor do I have any great or special interest in my past. Nor do I have a great deal of concern for my future."[26]

If Strawson is correct in his self-assessment, he lives very much in whatever his current project is. He attends to what he is doing without any concern for how it fits in with a larger plot or theme that would characterize his life. His projects do not need to find their way into a narrative whole. Strawson's attitude toward his own past is one of letting the dead bury the dead. And his attitude toward his future is that it is not yet his affair.

There is something Buddhist in Strawson's approach to his life. Buddhists advise living in the moment, in part as a way of letting go of worries about things one cannot control. For them, most humans live a suffering life. This is because we have all kinds of desires, and we worry about whether we can fulfill them. The trick to ending suffering, then, is to eliminate desire. Since desire is forward-looking, living in the moment will effectively eliminate desire. We will no longer be consumed with worry about whether our desires will be fulfilled. Instead, we can take pleasure in what is happening now, without asking whether it will lead toward something satisfying.

Strawson's view is like the Buddhist's in its concern for the present. He does not, however, place his view in the Buddhist tradition. It may be that he thinks that even a Buddhist life is too narratively structured for his taste. After all, the Buddhist can tell a story about herself that makes living in the present the proper approach for her to take toward herself and her world. She can explain how she came to realize that she was unhappy, and how she understood that her unhappiness had to do with her desires, and how this eventually led her to Buddhism. Strawson, in contrast, seems to do what he does without any concern for a story that would frame his doing it. This is not to say that he does whatever he likes. He probably has his own moral code that guides his choices. Whatever he chooses, however, is heedless of any relevance it might have for a narrative of his life. This is what he means by the term *Episodic*.

Strawson's view offers a challenge to those who want to think that the meaningfulness of life can be discerned in its narrative character. If meaningfulness required narrativity, then Strawson's life would be without meaning. Is this really what we want to say? It seems like a quick conclusion to draw, based simply on the fact that many other lives can be conceived narratively. If philosophy requires that we move slowly, then perhaps we need to linger over narrativity a bit more before making such a judgment.

There is another and deeper difficulty in ascribing meaningfulness to the narrative character of lives. Not all narratives seem to provide what we might want to call meaningfulness. Take the narrative of a depressed life. People who are chronically depressed often have a very coherent story to offer about their lives. It is a story in which they never get what they want, in which they are powerless to affect their world, and in which things always end badly, particularly for them. If the approach taken by narrative therapy is right, this story can become self-fulfilling: by telling this narrative to themselves, those who are depressed become people for whom things end badly. Moreover, if we look at people like this from the outside, the narrative they tell seems to have some basis in truth. We might say that the reason things don't work out for them is that they are depressed and therefore disengaged from their lives. But that does not contradict the fact, central to their understanding of their place in the world, that things do not work out for them.

People who are depressed or pessimistic or overly shy or

fearful often have a narrative character to their lives. Those lives are structured by stories with individual plots and particular themes. The plots concern their encounters with the world that usually end badly (or never really get started) in one way or another. The themes are of depression, pessimism, etc. But do those plots and those themes give their lives a sense of meaningfulness? It would seem rather that if their lives are meaningful, it is in spite of these themes rather than because of them. It is unclear how the very fact of having a narrative structure to one's life lends it meaning. Some narratives might seem to grant meaning to a life while others do not. If this is true, then why should we assume that the meaningfulness of a life lies in its narrative character? While it may be true that most human lives are structured narratively, that does not in itself seem to offer a clear path to understanding how those lives can be meaningful. If the idea of a narrative is to help us discover what might make our lives meaningful, it cannot be the bald fact of being able to tell stories about ourselves that does it.

Let us take stock. At the outset of this chapter, I said that human lives have trajectories. They arc from our birth to our death rather than being a jumble of unrelated moments. This suggests that in looking for what might make for a meaningful life we take a narrative approach. However, this approach runs into two problems. First, some lives are not lived narratively, which does not by itself seem to give us a reason to determine them as meaningless. Second, some lives that *are* lived narratively do not appear to be very meaningful; or at least if they are meaningful, their meaning does not lie in their narrative character. This poses a challenge. Is there something about the temporal (or narrative) character of our lives that can offer a source of meaningfulness that does not lie just in the temporality or narrativity itself? Can there instead be something that lies coiled inside our temporality or our narrativity that might answer to meaning? And can that something be had without defining a life like Strawson's as necessarily meaningless?

William Faulkner's great novel *The Sound and the Fury* concerns a decaying Southern family. The first three of the book's four parts are centered on different members of the damaged family. The first part is written from the point of view of Benjy, the family idiot—in Shakespeare's sense of the term *idiot*. ("It is a tale, told by an idiot, full of sound and fury, signifying nothing.") Benjy haunts golf courses, seeking for his vanished sister Caddie. He keeps hearing her name shouted when the golfers summon for their caddie, and thinks they are calling out to her. The second part, arguably even more difficult than the first, is told from the point of view of Quentin Compson, the family member who goes to Harvard and later commits suicide. Quentin is obsessed with family honor and the fall of the South. The third part turns to Jason Compson's point of view. He is a venal businessman, bitter at not being treated as well as either Quentin or Caddie. He blackmails his sister and keeps the child support payments Caddie sends to her daughter, who is living with Jason. All three of them—Benjy, Quentin, and Jason—are consumed in one way or another with their sister, Caddie, who is a constant presence in the novel although we never experience her from her own point of view.

An idiot, an obsessive suicidal intellectual, a mean-spirited businessman: the Compson family is not a prosperous one.

The final part is not written from a personal point of view. It is centered on the family maid, Dilsey. She is the glue that holds what is left of the household together. She brings Benjy to the black church, keeps Benjy's wayward caretaker Luster in line, cooks for Jason, maintains household order, and generally brings whatever stability there is in the declining Compson family. The final section of the novel, an appendix that traces the Compson family genealogy, ends with a two-word entry on Dilsey: "They endured."

If one were to describe the trajectory of Dilsey's life in a word, it would be *steadfast*. Dilsey is not oblivious to the disintegration around her. She recognizes the family situation clearly and soberly, and yet does not shy away from offering what support she can. She is not cowed by Jason's bullying, confronting him at one point: "You's a cold man, Jason, if man you is." She is not worn down by Luster's half-hearted caretaking of Benjy. When the novel discusses the early years of the Compson siblings, she is what she will be later: a blunt, persevering caregiver, looking toward her duties rather than, as the siblings do, personal obsessions or ghosts of the past.

Dilsey's steadfastness is sustained in the midst of a dying family. We admire her all the more for it, quixotic as it sometimes seems, inevitable as the downfall of the family is. Steadfastness, however, does not require such extreme circumstances in order to show itself. Parents who dedicate themselves to the well-being of their children, teachers who take as their goal year after year the flourishing of their students, athletes who devote themselves to their sport even as they grow older and slower or less agile, carpenters who seek over the course of decades to refine their craft: all of these people in one way or another exhibit the quality of steadfastness.

For them, as for Dilsey, steadfastness is a theme that characterizes their lives. It need not be the only theme, and for most flesh-and-blood characters, it likely is not. But it is something we admire about them. It gives their lives a certain heft. And it gives that heft not momentarily, but because they exhibit it across long stretches of their lives. It is a theme that characterizes their particular trajectories, a refrain that seems to lend their lives a certain value. We admire steadfastness in a life, which is why Faulkner could count on our sympathy with Dilsey in his portrayal of her.

Steadfastness is an example of what I want to call *narrative values of meaningfulness*, or *narrative values* for short. It is a theme that can characterize a life trajectory, or at least a large part of one. But it is not just a theme: it is also a value. Depression or fickleness are themes that can characterize the arc of a life, but we don't accord them any value. Lives are not enhanced in exemplifying these themes. What offers a sense of meaningfulness to particular themes is that they lend a certain kind of value to a life. The value that they add is that of meaningfulness.

There is much work to be done if I am to make the case that narrative values of meaningfulness offer the kind of objectivity that, combined with subjective engagement, can make a life meaningful. I need to say much more about this field of narrative values. It has not been discussed by philosophers, although I suspect that in our thinking about lives, many of us already have a sense—if an inchoate one—about these values. I must show why thinking in terms of narrative values doesn't face the difficulties that we saw with thinking in terms of narratives themselves, but I also must show why they allow us to see a life like Strawson's as potentially meaningful. I must contrast the field of narrative values with that of other types of value, especially moral value. And I must say why these values are objective in a way that still recognizes Camus's claim about the silence of the universe. Before embarking on these tasks, however, I should point out a way in which thinking in terms of narrative values shifts the ground of thinking about what can make a human life meaningful.

In the first chapter, during our initial search for the meaning of life, we found ourselves seeking a something, a meaning, a *what*. But steadfastness is not a *what*. It is a *how*. Steadfastness is a description of the way Dilsey goes about her life. There is not something out there called steadfastness that her life seeks to attain. There is no steadfastness etched into the universe that she achieves by her actions. Rather, we look at Dilsey's life and see that steadfastness is a theme depicting how she navigates her world. It is how she acts and reacts in the face of Benjy's limitations, Luster's juvenile behavior, Caddie's daughter's instability, and Jason's mercenary dishonesty.

In our search for meaningful living, we have too often been seduced by a false alternative. Either there is a meaning for human life inscribed in the universe, as Aristotle thought, or there is no such thing and we are bereft, as Camus thought. What both sides of this alternative agree on is that what makes life meaningful must be a meaning that exists, independent of us, and that for lives to be meaningful they must achieve or embody this meaning. However, the realm of narrative values suggests that a human life can be meaningful without attaining some sort of meaning. This is why, over the course of this book, I have gradually shifted from the term *meaning* to the term *meaningful*. What makes a life meaningful—or, more precisely, what answers to the objective side of meaningfulness—is not a thing to which it answers, but instead how it unfolds over the course of its time on the planet.

We can see this not only with steadfastness but with other narrative values as well. The guitarist Jimi Hendrix died from a drug overdose when he was twenty-seven. (Janis Joplin and Kurt Cobain also died at twenty-seven. What is it about rock stars at that age?) However, into his twenty-seven years he packed decades' worth of living. People who knew him describe him as someone who sought always to push the limits. Whatever they did—drugs, sex, other forms of experimentation— he did twice as much. At the fabled 1967 Monterey concert, there was an argument backstage about whether Hendrix would follow the Who onstage or vice versa. Given the power that each brought to the stage in their performances, neither wanted to be the next band up. Finally, Hendrix jumped on a chair, grabbed his guitar, and said that he would follow the Who, but that he was pulling out all the stops. His set turned out to be one of the most enduring in rock concert history, overwhelming in its fury and ending with his lighting his guitar on fire in a passion that might be described at once as religious, sexual, and demonic.

By all accounts, Hendrix's trajectory was characterized by what might be called a narrative value of intensity. His life was an investigation of how far one could press, how deeply one could experiment with oneself. In his life, and to an extent in many lives of rock stars of the 1960s as well as writers of the 1930s and 1940s, intensity became a signal value, drawing them toward experimentation and in the end toward excess. It marked their lives in ways that we might at some level feel ambivalent about but at another level admire. Intensity is the characteristic of a life of abandon, lived without fear and at times without restraint.

Intensity, of course, is a very different narrative value from steadfastness. In some ways, they may seem to be opposites. Intensity often requires release, while steadfastness usually prescribes abstinence. When we begin to reflect on the realm of narrative values, we see that there are many different ways to live meaningfully, not all of them in harmony with one another. This is not a problem. In painting, for instance, we may admire the dark colors of Rembrandt for their subtle expressiveness but also the vivid blues and yellows of Van Gogh for their dramatic ardor. It may be unlikely that one can live at once both intensely and steadfastly, but this does not diminish each as a narrative value, that is, a value that lends meaningfulness to a life.

Steadfastness, intensity, subtlety, adventurousness, intellectual curiosity, gracefulness, personal integrity, spontaneity, artistic or aesthetic creativity: all of these are themes that can characterize lives, expressions of the different yet meaningful ways that people can live. We might also include spirituality on this list. Living spiritually—living as though everything around one were sacred—is a narrative value that could lend meaning to a life. There are others as well. Aristotle listed twelve different virtues. Some of them might seem foreign to us now—for instance, temperance—or too weak to characterize a meaningful life—for instance, proper ambition as opposed to undue humility or vanity—but others seem fit to play the role of narrative values. Courage is certainly one. A courageous life is one we might admire not only as a morally worthy life but also a meaningful one. A courageous person who is subjectively engaged with his life in Wolf's or perhaps Haybron's sense would seem to be living a life we might want to characterize as meaningful.

Fannie Lou Hamer, a civil rights activist who never tired of her work no matter how many times she was beaten and jailed, is an exemplar of courage. During the 1964 Democratic Convention, at which Lyndon Johnson was trying to court Southern Democrats in order to ensure his election, Hamer briefly became famous when she led the integrated Mississippi Freedom Democratic Party that challenged the Democratic Party's seating of an all-white Mississippi delegation. The MFDP rejected a compromise that was agreed to by Martin Luther King, among others, that would only have allowed observer status for members of the MFDP. In 1968, however, she was seated as a member of the Mississippi delegation. Her commitment to civil rights and racial change never wavered. In later years, she worked for Head Start and as part of the Poor People's Campaign, subjectively engaged by her Christian faith and objectively displaying Aristotle's virtue of courage.

What goes for courage might also be said of others among Aristotle's list of virtues: sincerity, liberality, and to some lesser extent wittiness.

It is not surprising that Aristotle offers us narrative values. It was he, after all, who recognized that in judging a life we must look at its trajectory rather than at individual actions. While he saw the themes of that trajectory as in accord with a proper human life—a life ratified by the cosmos—we need not do so in order to draw upon him. There are ways of living that offer narrative meaningfulness without their having to be built into the structure of the universe. They are valuable ways of living, themes that offer a particular kind of worth, even if they do not reflect any ultimate telos of human existence.

To live in a way that expresses a narrative value, however, is not to live that way in some small corner of one's existence. A steadfast life is not one that is steadfast only in one arena. One can be loyal to a friend or lover, and can be so over the course of decades, without being steadfast in the way Dilsey was. Her steadfastness was expressed in various aspects of her life. Her constancy, her "endurance" as Faulkner has it, found its way into her interaction with everyone around her. If, by contrast, we imagine someone who betrays everyone they know except their lover or their mother, we would not want to call such a life steadfast. It might be loyal to someone, but someone who heard the overall story of that life would not be tempted to think of it as steadfast. To be steadfast, or to be intense, or to express any other narrative value, is to act in a way that exhibits that value across various aspects of one's life, and over a good portion of one's existence.

In this way, we can see how a religious life can be meaningful even if God is not the source of its meaning. In the first chapter, I denied that we can rely on God to be the source of the meaningfulness of life because, among other reasons, we have to decide what meaningfulness is before we can say that God gives it to us. This was like the dilemma regarding the good. If the good is only what God declares to be good, then God could declare slavery to be good and that would make it so. But if God can't do that, there has to be a standard of the good independent of God to which God must live up if he/she/it is to be good. This might seem to imply that there is no relation between a religious life and a meaningful one.

But this isn't so. A life of steadfast devotion to God can be meaningful precisely in its steadfastness, or in the spirituality it lends to a life. It doesn't have to be God that grants the meaningfulness to a religious life; instead, it can be the way a religious life is undertaken. There is something compelling, even to many nonbelievers, about the life of a nun or a religious ascetic. That degree and sustained ardor of devotion can be inspiring not only to those who share a particular faith—for whom it is often meant to provide a model—but also for those who don't. For my own part, I am as atheist as the day is long, but I am fascinated by Trappist monks or Trappistine nuns, who speak only when necessary and in some cases not at all. This expresses a level of commitment that commands my admiration even though I deny the existence of the object of that commitment. While Dilsey touches me through her expression of steadfastness in relations with others, the religious ascetic does so in her steadfastness in relation to God. (There is, I think, a lesson to be drawn here about how the acknowledgment of narrative values can promote mutual respect among those with different religious views.)

One might ask, at this point, whether one needs to know that one is expressing a narrative value in order to do so. Are narrative values things we reflect on and then cultivate? Must we direct our lives in accordance with them in order to be said to express them?

If that were true, narrative values would be found in very few lives. It is unclear, and perhaps unlikely, that Fannie Lou Hamer told herself that she was living courageously or that Jimi Hendrix saw himself as expressing intensity in his experimentation, or that many of us reflect on the narrative values that might or might not inform our lives. Instead, Hamer was focused on what needed to be done, and Hendrix on what offered itself to be done. It is not impossible that Hamer might, in a moment of fear, have asked herself what a person of real courage would have done. But for her life to be one of courage did not require it. It required only that she live in a way that would be recognized as courageous.

The realm of narrative values provides standards to assess the meaningfulness of lives, of one's own or another's. It might, but need not, be reflected on in one's own life. This is what it is to be an objective standard. It can be helpful to reflect on this realm, particularly when one is wondering about the meaningfulness of one's own life. It offers a framework for reflection in those moments of doubt when we wonder what our life amounts to. And it provides guidance for those who admire certain narrative values and seek to express them in their lives. Someone's trajectory can express a narrative value, however, without their being aware of it.

In fact, since narrative values are objective rather than subjective, it is even possible that some people could be mistaken about the narrative values they express. They might try to express one narrative value, but wind up expressing another. For instance, suppose one thought that his life was an exercise in subtlety, but the qualities he exhibited in that life had more to do with steadfastness in his relationships. I once had an uncle like this. He thought of himself as clever in conversation in a subtle way. For example, he thought verbal puns were the height of intellectual cleverness. He also considered himself capable of giving signals to others of his appreciation of them, but again in a subtle way. He would offer winks and nods that were meant for particular people but that everyone noticed. All of this was obvious in a way that for some reason eluded him. And because he was so kind to the rest of the family nobody wanted to disabuse him of illusions of subtlety. We were, perhaps, a bit patronizing with him, but the affection all around seemed more important to the rest of us than making him self-conscious about his behavior.

Of course, my uncle never said to himself that he was expressing a *narrative value*. My uncle did not think in terms of narrative values. Given that I have never seen the concept invoked in relation to people's lives, I suspect that very few people have thought of human lives in terms of narrative values. But he did think of himself as subtle, and would periodically tell one or another of us of this—in, of course, a very unsubtle way.

Our reflection on the realm of narrative values so far might leave either of two misimpressions that should be corrected before we go any farther. The first is that the existence of narrative values in a life is binary: either one's life is exhibiting a narrative value or it is not. This in turn would lead to the idea that a life is either objectively meaningful or it is not. We should not think of narrative values this way. Rather than being binary, narrative values are a matter of the more and the less. Lives can be more or less intense, more or less steadfast, or curious, or spontaneous, or courageous, or subtle (except perhaps for my uncle, who wasn't subtle at all). Most lives are probably more like this than like the exemplars we have considered here. Very few people live as intensely as Jimi Hendrix did, but this does not mean that their lives do not express intensity. Most people who, say, are deeply engaged by their work, seeking to develop its possibilities or create something new with it, express a degree of intensity. It may not be a central theme in their lives, but the more important a theme it is, the more meaningful their lives become in that way.

The other possible misimpression that should be corrected would be that lives can only express a single narrative value. We have focused on particular values associated with particular people. But most lives are more complex than that. To be sure, there are some people wholly dedicated to a task or a way of living that expresses a particular narrative value. Dilsey was like that. Hendrix may or may not have been like that, but the story of his life that has come down to us paints that picture. Another paragon of intensity (although intense steadfastness might better capture him) is the saxophonist John Coltrane. Coltrane was so dedicated to his instrument that he would become excited at the prospect of new scales to practice. Once he was asked what he would do if he were not playing the saxophone. His reply was that he didn't know how to do anything else. (Coltrane's work, particularly his later work like *A Love Supreme*, also could stand as a testimony to the narrative value of spirituality that began to infuse his life.)

Most of us aren't like this, however. For my own part, I admire people so taken up by what they do that they cannot see themselves doing anything else. The philosophers I read, the music I listen to, many of the people I like to hang out with and learn from, are consumed by a single thought or style or goal. Although I like to live intensely, my own approach is more of a serial intensity, delving into one thing for a while, and then another. Perhaps I am more curious than intense (or, if I am deceiving myself here, more fickle than curious). In any event, most lives are not lived with a single overarching dedication to a particular task or goal or practice.

The lack of an overarching narrative value does not force us to conclude that our lives do not express any narrative values. They may express several values to one degree or another. Imagine the fortunate soul who has a career that affords her creativity, worthy friends with whom she is steadfast, and an outside interest, say competitive swimming, that she passionately loves. Perhaps these various projects are each so significant in her life that periodically there are tensions between them. Nevertheless, she is focused enough to balance them, if at moments at a precarious perch. The creativity does not flag at work, the friends retain her loyalty (without her having to betray others), and she swims with abandon in her free time: and she has been at all of these for much of her adulthood. This person expresses several narrative values. She is not consumed by an instrument in the way Coltrane was. She is not rendered as stubbornly dedicated to holding together a dying family as Faulkner did with Dilsey. The world will likely not hear of her in the way it hears of those whose single-minded commitments lead them to write a great novel or excel in sport or develop a new technology. Nevertheless her life expresses narrative values, as do the lives of many of us. We often express more than one and usually far less prominently than Coltrane or Dilsey or Hendrix or Fannie Lou Hamer. But they do weave their way, in soft rather than bright colors, through the routes many of us trace.

Once we correct these possible misimpressions, once we recognize that narrative values are not binary and that lives can encompass more than one, we understand that the assessment of narrative values—in our own lives or in those of others—is rarely a simple affair. It requires perception, reflection, weighing, and judgment. Lives do not come with narrative labels attached. But isn't this as it should be? After all, we have been asking about what makes a human life meaningful—or at least the objective side of a meaningful life. We should not expect it to be simple. The complexity of judgment should reflect the complexity of living. And for most of us, our existence is fraught with ambivalences, with change, with dead periods, with uncertainty. It might even be that there is a conflict in our lives among narrative values, that, for instance, we value both spirituality and intensity, and that while the former leads us to seek a certain peacefulness with the world, the other leads us toward potential conflict. Assessing a theme or several themes in a life involves getting a sense of what has dominated over the course of many years. It obliges one to separate what seems truly characteristic of a life from what is passing, the signal from the noise. This is no easy task, particularly for one's own life. And in most cases it is one's own life that is the object of reflection about meaningfulness. But in cases where one is asking about the meaningfulness of one's life, the difficulty of the task can be matched by its urgency. There are those among us who, without reflection or soul searching, without lying awake at night wondering whether we amount to anything, express narrative values in the way we navigate the world. But most of us are not like this. We ask, we doubt, we seek a way of understanding ourselves that will tell us whether we are somehow on track. And for us, the difficulty of the task does not daunt. Rather, it challenges us.

If the proposal I have made is right—and so far it is only a proposal—then it addresses the dilemma we saw above between finding something about the trajectory of a life that can offer meaningfulness and not saying that a non-narrative life like Strawson's must lack meaning. The difficulty with embracing narrativity itself, in addition to Strawson's challenge, is that not all narratives seem to provide a sense of meaningfulness. But if we think in terms of narrative *values* rather than just narratives, we overcome that difficulty. Depression, fickleness, disempowerment: these themes do not lend meaning to a life because they are not values. If we want a term to contrast them with narrative values, we might call them narrative *dis-*

values. They withdraw rather than add value to the arc of a person's life. In approaching a life by way of narrative values, then, we find that the meaningfulness does not lie in the narrative itself. Instead we are asking whether that narrative is characterized by or expresses a theme that would give it value.

Seen this way, even Strawson's antinarrative life might express a narrative value. After all, his claim is not that his life does not take place over time. He does not deny that it arcs from birth to death. He has no interest in his past or his future, but he does not say that it has neither past nor future. Rather, he resists the idea that his past and future are woven together with his present in anything that would form a story line. As he puts it, his life is Episodic rather than Diachronic.

What narrative value or values might such a life express? Strawson does not tell us much about his life, so we can only speculate here. Suppose that, heedless of his past commitments, he throws himself into different projects as they interest him, experimenting with and engaging in these projects that take him far from where he has been before. And suppose that he doesn't just dip his toes into these projects but instead throws himself into them until they reach some sort of completion. Then we might say that his life is an adventurous one. Or we might imagine something different. We can fancy instead that, since he is unconcerned with his past, unbeknownst to him he has always been circling around the same philosophical questions, thinking about issues from different angles but always coming back to the same problems, shedding new and different light upon them. It might be that, though Episodic, his life is nevertheless steadfast in its attention to a small range of important philosophical concerns. We can picture him as the Dilsey of this or that philosophical question. And given the tone of his article, of which my citations only give a glimpse, it is not hard to imagine him this way, as an impatient and at times intolerant but steadfast thinker.

What Strawson objects to in narrativity is story or plot.[27] Narrative values are not concerned with story or plot. They are concerned with theme. A human life can express a theme without seeking to, and without that theme's requiring a particular narrative coherence to its plot. What a narrative value requires is a valuable motif that can be discerned, by oneself or another, in the complex unfolding experience of living. That can happen in the absence of the kind of biography that offends Strawson's Episodic sensibilities.

The realm of narrative values seems to offer us a way to think about what might make a life meaningful without the difficulties associated with narratives themselves. It constitutes a realm of value that has seemed to elude philosophical reflection. Philosophers think of moral value and aesthetic value and personal value, but not narrative value—at least as it concerns living. If narrative values are considered, they would be a subset of aesthetic values, applied to aesthetic objects like novels. But, as the historian and philosopher Michel Foucault has observed, "What strikes me is the fact that in our society, art has become something which is related only to objects and not to individuals, or to life. That art is something which is specialized or which is done by experts who are artists. But couldn't everyone's life become a work of art? Why should the lamp or the house be an art object, but not our life?"[28]

Lives that express narrative values can be interesting or beautiful or compelling. And because of this, we are drawn to them. We are drawn to those who live them, and in some instances to living them ourselves. Narrative values give a sense (or senses) of coherence to a life. But they do more than that. As we have seen, a life can cohere in a way that does not lend it value. What narrative values capture is our sense that certain themes characterizing human trajectories lend them a kind of richness or significance. They are rich or significant in a way that is not moral and yet more than merely satisfying to the person whose trajectory it is. We might say that narrative values illuminate styles of lives that are worth living. Another way to say these styles are worth living is to say that they lend something meaningful to a life. Narrative values, in this sense, are ways in which human life can be meaningful. They may not be the only ways. But in the silent universe we share with Camus, to discover at least some ways in which life can be meaningful is, for most of us who seek a sense of significance to our lives, to discern the outlines of the shapes our lives can take. And in taking one or another of these shapes, perhaps we might avoid the fate of looking back upon our lives with a sense of desolation.

Of course, we might not always know that the reason we are attracted to certain lives, or seek to live them ourselves, is that they express particular narrative values. Just as we can be drawn to a piece of music, or a lamp or a house, we can be drawn to styles of living without reflecting on the reasons for it. And among those reasons can be that they are adventurous or intellectually curious or, as in the lives that intrigue me, steadfast in their commitment to a worthwhile project. Not all of us, of course, are compelled by expressions of the same narrative values. But someone can recognize the value of, say, subtlety without being drawn to it herself, just as one can recognize classical music or impressionist painting as worthy without being gripped by them.

However, doesn't all of this make narrative values too subjective? If something's being a value depends on my recognizing it as a value, doesn't this mean that the values depend on me? Isn't the decision about whether intensity is a narrative value simply mine to make? And even if I recognize something as a narrative value, might not the decision about whether a particular life expresses that value lie with me? Doesn't the judgment about whether my life is an intense one rest on its feeling intense, regardless of what anybody else thinks about it? And, in the end, aren't we all the arbiters of narrative values, in our own case and in our judgments of others?

There is a deep issue here about what makes a value objective. It concerns the question of whether there can be any objectivity that is more than individual judgment, that is, whether in the case of values there can be any objectivity at all. To answer that question will take an entire chapter—in our case the fifth chapter—to unfold. However, at the moment we can at least give a breezy plausibility to the idea that it isn't merely up to the person living the life to decide whether it expresses a particular narrative value. People can be mistaken in their ascription of narrative values, either to themselves or to others.

Let's look first at intensity. Suppose that someone thinks he is living an intense life of following sports on television. For those of us who are devoted fans of a team, it can certainly *feel* intense to watch one's team on television. And now that there are so many media outlets, it is possible to keep up with a team's progress—its trades, its hiring and firing of coaches, its recruiting prospects, speculation as to its future standing—even during the off-season. In my hometown of Clemson, South Carolina, there is a radio station where one can discuss Clemson's football team all year around with many of the hosts and announcers.

Wouldn't such a life count as an intense one? It certainly might seem so to the person living it. After a close football game, many people here in Clemson will describe it by talking about how *intense* it was. I can imagine that feeling could be addictive. A close win in a crucial game is something one wants to remember and relive. (I am not entirely immune to this feeling. When I recall how the injured New York Knicks center Willis Reed came out to the court in the final seconds before the beginning of the deciding playoff game with the Los Angeles Lakers in 1970, I still get a little misty-eyed. And that was over forty years ago.) Among intense lives, couldn't one be where someone successfully cultivated those feelings of fan intensity?

And if this is so, might we not imagine that, under certain circumstances, the life of Mary with her goldfish that we discussed in the previous chapter would also count as intense? Suppose she felt intensely about her goldfish and her relation to her goldfish, that her obsession was not debilitating but intense, giving her a feeling of being keenly alive. Wouldn't that make her life an intense one?

But if Mary's life, intensely felt, can embody the narrative value of intensity, then we have a problem. Recall the reason we imagined Mary's life in the first place: to show that subjective engagement alone cannot guarantee meaningfulness. Susan Wolf utilizes the example of Mary (although not so christened) to show that in order for a life to be meaningful, "subjective attraction" by itself is insufficient. That attraction must meet "objective attractiveness" in order for a life to be meaningful. Happiness, or even deep engagement, is not enough. The point of appealing to the realm of narrative values is to offer a candidate for objective attractiveness. This candidate, while different from traditional conceptions of what makes a life meaningful, is supposed to offer a way to conceive of meaningfulness so that we can know what is lacking in a life like Mary's.

However, if Mary's life can count as expressing the narrative value of intensity, then narrative values will not fill the bill. The reason is that, as philosophers might put it, the purported objectivity of narrative values reduces to subjectivity. That is, intensity would be nothing more than *felt* intensity. What would make a life intense would simply be that it lent a sense of intensity to the person living it. Narrative values—in this case the narrative value of intensity—would not be a matter of objective attractiveness but instead just a form of subjective attraction. If Mary's life and that of the football fan can be described as narratively intense, and this because they experienced their lives as intense, then perhaps narrative values don't really give us the objectivity we need in order to have an adequate conception of meaningfulness. We are right back where we were at the end of the previous chapter.

A first reaction to this difficulty might be to think of it as a local one. Perhaps the problem is not with the realm of narrative values, but only with intensity itself. If so, then we can abandon intensity as a narrative value and see whether other values would serve us better. But this is too quick. I think that intensity is a good example, not only of a narrative value but of why narrative values aren't reducible to subjective attractiveness.

To say that a person lives a narratively intense life is not simply to claim that it feels intense to the person whose life it is. It is to characterize how she goes about living that life. It is to claim that she throws herself into what she does with abandon; that she displays evidence of intense involvement through corporeal expression, time spent engaged in her projects, discussion or thought about her projects even when not directly participating in them. To be intensely involved is to have the gears of one's activity mesh with those of one's projects in a particularly tight fit.

Think of the difference between Mary or the football fan and Jimi Hendrix. Or better, think of the difference between Hendrix and one of his own fans. Both might have felt intensely during one of his concerts, but only one of them was living that intensity. Hendrix was involved in a project of creating music that he threw himself into. It wasn't something he watched; it was something he did. And he did it not only at that moment but at other moments when he practiced his music, thought about it, learned new techniques by watching fellow musicians, and experimented with all this during other concerts. For someone's life to be characterized by a narrative value like intensity, it is not felt (or not only felt), but expressed. It is lived. The Hendrix fan is not living intensity; he is watching Hendrix live it, and perhaps himself experiencing it vicariously.

This does not mean, of course, that the fan's life is meaningless. It only means that, inasmuch as he is a fan, he is not expressing the narrative value of intensity.

Intensity, as a narrative value rather than a feeling, characterizes the way one goes about one's life. It is a theme that is expressed not only in what one experiences but in the manner in which one engages with one's activities. Narrative values are not a spectator sport. They are a matter of activity rather than passivity.

This is true even in cases where there seems to be no activity involved. Recall the Trappist monks, who speak only when necessary or not at all. It might appear that they are not doing anything; after all, they are refraining from speech. But this abstention is not a passive one. They are not asleep, nor are they simply sitting and staring into space or watching others practice a craft. Their silence is a form of engagement with the world and with God. It is an active restraint, an element in a steadfast commitment to their religious beliefs. Contrast this with the felt intensity of the Hendrix fan. He is not living his experienced intensity. Hendrix is living it. In that sense, intensity does not characterize what the fan does, but how he feels about what someone else is doing.

We can see also this difference if we recall my uncle, who experienced himself as subtle although he was far from it. The difference between being subtle and experiencing oneself as subtle is like the difference between lived and felt intensity. Italo Calvino's novel *Invisible Cities* consists mostly in imagined conversations between Marco Polo and Kublai Khan in which Polo describes various cities he has visited. Each city is defined by a single characteristic. As the novel unfolds, it becomes evident that the characteristics embodied by the cities are not features of particular cities but aspects of our humanity. Marco Polo, in exploring different cities, reveals facets of human existence: longing, fantasy, eternal disappointment, a desire to erase the past, the fragility of memory, the passing of novelty. "Soon the city fades before your eyes, the rose windows are expunged, the statues on the corbels, the domes.... Millions of eyes look up at windows, bridges, capers, and they might be scanning a blank page. Many are the cities like Phyllis, which elude the gaze of all, except the man who catches them by surprise."[29]

Calvino's Marco Polo is a subtle reader of humanity. When

he visits a city he does not just see its outward appearance. He peers into its soul. And in discovering the soul of a city he discovers something about the human soul. He does not investigate himself and decide that he is subtle; nor does he exhibit a sense of his own subtlety. Instead he is caught up in his reflections and in his conversation with Kublai Khan. His is a lived subtlety that contrasts with my uncle's experienced subtlety, a narrative expression of subtlety rather than a feeling that one is being subtle.

We can see the same distinction if we reflect on adventurousness. Ishmael, the narrator in Herman Melville's *Moby-Dick*, joins the doomed whaling expedition because "Whenever I find myself growing grim about the mouth; whenever it is a damp, drizzly November in my soul . . . then I account it high time to get to sea as soon as I can."[30] In order to be adventurous, one has to get wide of one's current life in ways that involve making oneself vulnerable to pain, humiliation, exposure, or something of the kind. A life of adventure requires challenging oneself, resisting urges toward complacency, laying oneself open to an uncertain future.

This is why a life of shopping, whatever its other merits, is not one of adventure. It might feel adventurous to try on new clothes and to imagine different personas associated with different outfits. But this would be only the imagination of adventure, not an expression of the narrative value of adventure. Perhaps, if the shopper were someone who periodically bought a new wardrobe, utterly distinct from the previous one, and then sought to live according to it, and if the different wardrobes represented entirely different lifestyles, then we might have at least the beginnings of a more adventurous life. (One of my professors in graduate school would travel to

Paris every summer to have dinner with a friend of his. Unknown to this friend, the first place the friend mentioned in conversation my professor would then go to, no matter where it was. Then he would travel from there, often not knowing where he would go next. He was described by everyone who knew him as, among other things, adventurous.) But shopping itself, no matter how much of a thrill it gives the shopper, will never be an exercise in adventure. In fact, as a rule of thumb we can probably say that shopping malls are not promising venues for the appearance of the narrative value of adventurousness.

Intensity, subtlety, adventurousness: these are not (or not merely) experienced themes, but rather lived ones. They characterize ways in which people might craft the temporal arc of their days. They are, as we have seen, only one side of a meaningful life. For a life to be meaningful, it also must possess a sense of subjective engagement, of something akin to happiness in the resonant way Daniel Haybron has described it. However, lived themes are distinct from that subjective engagement. There is a difference between thinking or feeling that one is expressing a narrative value and actually doing so.

For some, there may seem to be a value that I have missed that would lend objective meaning to a life: love. Is love a narrative value? And if not, is it some sort of other value that would lend a life meaningfulness?

The question of what love is and its role in our lives is, as you will surely have guessed, a vexed one.[31] Is love an emotion, something that lies inside us? Or is it a relation between two people? Is it rational or irrational? Does one love individuals or qualities of individuals? How should we conceive love? And if we can't say what love is, how are we to understand it in relation to narrative values specifically and the meaningfulness of a life more generally?

I cannot, of course, offer you a compelling account of the nature of love. I have spent some time studying it (yes, philosophically as well as experientially), and know that I am not in a position to resolve the various debates it has engendered. Even if I could, it would take another book alongside this one to do so. But I can at least gesture in a couple of directions that would allow love to be integrated into the account of meaningfulness being constructed here.

First, on the subjective side. To the extent that love is an emotion or a feeling, it seems to display, or at least reinforce, the characteristics of happiness that Daniel Haybron has laid out: attunement, engagement, and endorsement. In fact, some people might argue that love is one of the central sources of happiness, and that it would be difficult to imagine a happy life that did not involve feelings of love. If that is so, then love would be necessary at least for happiness, if not for meaningfulness. And to the extent to which love was necessary for an engagement in one's life, it would be required for a meaningful life as well.

From the objective side, love is associated with narrative values like steadfastness and intensity, and more indirectly with values like courage. Although it is possible to express these values without the existence of love, love is perhaps one of the most important motivators for such expression. And to that degree, even if love is not itself a narrative value (something we could not decide without solving the question of what love is), it is deeply tied to narrative values and their appearance in our lives. And if love is tied to both narrative values and to subjective engagement, then love, whatever it may be, is implicated—at least indirectly—in the meaningfulness of many lives.

At this point, however, some readers might object to the appeal to narrative values as grounding for the objective attractiveness of a life. In the previous chapter, I addressed the concern that having objective criteria for meaningfulness might unfairly yield judgments that certain lives were less meaningful than others. There I said that potential judgments of meaninglessness (or at least less meaningfulness) were the price that must be paid for being able to answer the question of meaning. A similar, although distinct, worry might arise regarding narrative values. At a first go, we might put the worry this way: does the appeal to narrative values as an answer to the question of meaningfulness vitiate the particular individuality of our lives?

We like to see ourselves as unique individuals. Each of us hopes that our life provides a singular and perhaps incomparable approach to the possibilities of human existence. To find that another person has duplicated our history—our interests, our relationships, our activities, our emotions—would be devastating. In philosophy, there are many thought experiments that are done with imagined duplicates. They all carry with them a haunting sense of personal loss. Imagining that I have a double somewhere undermines my distinctiveness as a person and leaves me feeling impoverished. It is important to each of us to have a sense of irreplaceability.

The objection some readers might have to using narrative values as an objective standard for meaningfulness is that it subverts that individuality. If what renders a life meaningful (alongside subjective engagement) is that it is subtle or intellectually curious or displays personal integrity or courage, then the meaningfulness of a life seems to be nothing more than an example of a general narrative value. As far as meaning goes, there is no difference between Dilsey's steadfastness and that of a Trappist monk. They are both just instances of steadfastness. And doesn't that dissolve the individuality of each person into the generality of a narrative value? The meaningfulness of a life does not lie in the particularity of the way it is lived but rather only in its expression of the generic and abstract standard of steadfastness, courage, or some other category.

There is an affinity between this concern and the earlier one regarding whether objectivity should matter at all for meaningfulness. Both of them are worries about the specific character of individuals. The first worry focuses on whether objective judgment renders certain lives less meaningful, while the second worry centers on whether the kinds of judgment associated with narrative values erases the individuality of certain lives. The difference between them lies in this: the second concern grants that there can be judgments of meaningfulness but is fearful that grounding those judgments in a set of general categories like narrative values abolishes the importance of our personal particularity. Even if there must be objectivity, it asks, does that objectivity need to lie in something as divorced from the details of a person's life as a narrative value?

Once we recognize what the worry is, we can see that it is not simply about narrative values. It is instead about using *any* general categories to assess the meaningfulness of a life. The problem with narrative values seems to be not that they are narrative values, but that they are trying to force particular lives into global categories. Shouldn't the meaningfulness of a life instead be grounded in the specific trajectory of that life rather than its display of a more general standard? Shouldn't what makes my life meaningful, to the extent that it is meaningful, be something about *my particular life* as distinct from the lives of others?

If we follow this line of thought, then we wind up, as with the earlier objection, unable to offer any standards for objectivity. A standard, as we have seen, is a criterion to compare something to, whether it is a life trajectory or a test performance or a race result. In order for it to be a standard, it cannot be reducible to a particular life or performance or race, but must be a general category that can be applied to more than one instance. That is part of what gives it its objectivity. If the meaningfulness of a life must be grounded in the particularity of that life, then we would have no way of saying whether it met an objective standard.

To see why, consider an example. Suppose I said that what made Hendrix's life meaningful was not its intensity, but the particular way he went about it. Now someone might ask what this particular way was. The answer might be something involving Hendrix's style: his style of dress, of playing guitar, of being with those around him, even his style of walking down the street. But this leads to the question of what it was about his style that rendered it meaningful. Here there are two possible types of responses. I could say that his style was memorable or interesting or something like that. But this type of response brings us back to general categories. After all, there are other people whose style might be memorable or interesting or something like that. Saying that Hendrix's style was memorable does not capture the particularity of his style. Instead, it sees that style in terms of a more general classification. But that's what narrative values do. So this type of response does not get us around the problem.

The other possible response is to deny that it is in terms of a general category that his style is meaningful. It is not that Hendrix's style is memorable or interesting that makes it meaningful, but just that it is . . . well, this particular style. To see what his style is, one has to look at it, encounter it—in his case through films and recordings.

There is certainly something to the idea that people's personal styles are an important aspect of who they are. Think of a person's voice. We immediately recognize people by their voices, and the voice of a friend or a loved one is almost always comforting. There is perhaps nothing as individual as a voice. It is part of what makes a person the person they are. And if one is asked about the quality or the character of someone's voice, there is nothing to say that will capture it in its uniqueness. One can only respond to a request like that by saying, "Listen."

Someone's voice, or more broadly their style, is part of their individual character. But is it what gives their life meaning? More pointedly, does it provide an objective standard for meaning? What we are seeking is a way of thinking about our lives against which we can measure them, in order to ask ourselves from a particular angle whether our lives have been worthwhile and how to make them worthwhile. We hope that the standard we discover will be both wide enough to encompass many different lives and yet rigorous enough to provide a real measure. If it's not wide enough then few lives will wind up being meaningful. If it's not rigorous enough then we are left without any guidance.

The problem with resting the meaningfulness of a person's life on their particular style is that it offers no guidance. It is without rigor, because it is without standards. If one asks what makes Hendrix's style or my friend's voice meaningful, there is nothing to say, because anything one says will involve a general category like that of narrative values. If someone asks what it is about my friend's voice that lends meaning to his life, my reply of "Listen," is not an answer. To be sure, a reply like that might indicate how much I value my friend. It suggests how much my friend means to me. But to say that my friend means a lot to me is not to say that my friend's life is meaningful on its own terms. And what we are looking for is the latter rather than the former. We're interested in what makes a life meaningful in itself, not meaningful in the sense of important to others.

If we are to have an objective standard for meaningfulness, we need general categories of some sort. We cannot just baldly appeal to the particularities of a person's life. But this should not concern those who worry that we lose a person's uniqueness in appealing to narrative values. There are two reasons for this. First, the judgment of narrative values does indeed refer to the particularities of a person's life. But it does not rest there. It is in terms of the particular path, what we have called the arc of a person's life, that we ask about narrative values. Dilsey's life and that of the Trappist monk might both be steadfast. But it is because of Dilsey's unique relationship to the Compson family that her life is so, and it is because of the Trappist monk's relation to God that his life is so. The narrative value may be general, something that can be seen in a diversity of lives. It is seen, however, in the particularity of each of those different lives. The uniqueness of a life is not lost when we ask about what narrative value or values it might express. Rather, the judgment of meaningfulness is made by reference both to the realm of narrative values *and* to the unique trajectory of the life in question.

For most of us the life that is in question is our own. It is rarely urgent for us to ask whether another's life is meaningful. Most often, it happens when a friend or family member is depressed or in doubt about who they are or where they are headed. But when I lie awake at night and ask about the worthwhileness of life, it is not my friend's or my wife's or children's I'm asking about. It is my own. And even when I do puzzle over the worthwhileness of life in general, what I'm after are not judgments of other people's lives, but instead the comfort of knowing that there are standards, that human life is not without significance, that Camus was too quick to despair.

The second reason we should not worry that the general category of narrative values will abolish a person's uniqueness is that judgments of meaningfulness are only one kind of judgment someone can make about a life. Meaningfulness is not all there is to a life. To ask whether or to what extent my life is a meaningful one does not exhaust the issue of its value. There are other types of value that a human life can express.

This may sound strange. After all, we might want to say, if one's life is without meaning (or at least has very little), then what kind of value could it have? Isn't a meaningless life a worthless one, one that is futile to continue? Indeed, isn't it the point of asking about the meaningfulness of a life that we want to find some reason to go on, some reason, as Camus has it, not to commit suicide?

In asking these questions, there is an assumption that we need to abandon if we are to see narrative values as offering a sense of meaningfulness to life. It is the assumption that at bottom, the only important question about our lives is whether they are meaningful. We can see this assumption at work in the views we discussed in the first chapter.

Recall that for Aristotle the question was not that of a meaningful life but rather of a good life. Nevertheless, his idea that a good human life is one whose contours are inscribed in the cosmos is very close to our idea of a meaningful life. For Aristotle, as for us, if a human life is to be a proper human life, it must be guaranteed somehow by the universe. For our own part, we tend to substitute God for Aristotle's idea of the cosmos, but the idea is the same. God is the guarantor of the meaningfulness of human life. We are all part of God's plan.

As we saw, however, God cannot underwrite meaning. Meaningfulness, like goodness, must be decided by us before we can ascribe it to God or God's plan. That is the source of Camus's anguish. The universe is silent regarding meaning. If we make it up, it is only our doing. And a universe bereft of the promise of meaning threatens to be an intolerable universe in which to soldier on.

The line of thought from Aristotle through religion to Camus makes of meaningfulness the sole criterion of the worth of human endeavor. Either the universe gives us a message of meaningfulness and we have reason to continue to live, or it does not and then we do not. Meaning becomes the centerpiece of human existence.

If we follow the path marked out by Susan Wolf in the previous chapter, we need not hew to this either/or. Meaningfulness is one kind of value a human life can have or express. But it need not be the only one. What makes a life worthwhile might be its meaningfulness. And for it to *feel* worthwhile to me it might be necessary that it has some sort of meaningfulness. However, this need not be all. Most important, human lives can be not only meaningful but good. Wolf distinguishes the meaningful from the good—as she does from the happy.

This is not a trivial distinction. The meaningfulness attested to by narrative values is one way a human life can be valuable. Moral goodness is another. (And just being human, or being alive, can itself be yet another.) Moreover, the particularity of human lives allows for different balances between meaningfulness and goodness. A life can be meaningful in certain ways and good in others, and the balance between these depends in large part on the specific character of that life.

If we divorce the question of the meaningfulness of a life from that of the value of a life in general, then we can see that narrative values don't exhaust the significance of living. The realm of narrative values does not encompass all that can be said of the worthiness of a person's singular trajectory. We need not, then, worry that narrative values will betray the specificity of people's lives. Not only do we need to see narrative values in that specificity; we can recognize that there is more to be said about the specificity of a human life than just that it is meaningful.

This raises a question for us. If human lives can be meaningful, and if alternatively they can be morally good, and if meaningfulness is not necessarily moral goodness, then what is the relation between them? Meaningfulness is a certain kind of value that a human trajectory can express, and moral goodness another. What is a meaningful life if it is not a good one? And what is the relationship between meaning and morality? What, if anything, do narrative values have to do with moral values?

Chapter Four

MEANINGFUL LIVES, GOOD LIVES, BEAUTIFUL LIVES

Henry James's *The Portrait of a Lady* is a study of womanhood in late nineteenth-century Europe. Like his brother, the famous psychologist and philosopher William James, Henry was an acute observer of human character. The lady of the title, Isabel Archer, goes from America to Europe, eventually marries, and settles in Rome. Among the people she meets is her cousin Ralph Touchett. Ralph is physically weak with a debilitating lung disease. He is in love with his cousin, but doesn't believe he deserves her because of his feeble constitution. As he puts it to Isabel, his love for her is "without hope." Throughout the novel, he seeks to support her, first by convincing his father to leave her a fortune upon the father's death, then by giving her sage advice, which in the case of marriage she ignores to her own peril. Near death, he travels from his home in England to Rome, where Isabel lives, in order to be near her. The final favor he does for her is unintended. He returns to England to die, where, in defiance of her husband, she visits him. This allows her an independence she had not previously achieved from her tormented marriage.

Ralph is not altruistic, nor is he selfless. He is, however, steadfast in his love for Isabel, as he was in his care for his father. His ironic and sometimes sardonic humor allows him to keep a distance from his emotions, particularly when he is with those he cherishes. One of the few times he confronts a situation directly, advising Isabel against marrying Gilbert Osmond, he wonders afterward whether he made a mistake in being forthright. Perhaps, he thinks, if he had held his tongue she would not have shut him out after her marriage and he could have been more support to her in what was, as he predicted, a disastrous union.

Ralph Touchett is a good man in a straightforwardly moral sense. He also embodies the narrative value of steadfastness. He is not, however, a happy man. He is remote from his emotions, believing himself unworthy of their satisfaction. He chalks this up to his physical condition. It seems, though, that his condition is less the cause of his remoteness than the excuse for it. Had he not been plagued by a lung disease, he would have found some other reason to keep his emotional distance, from himself as well as others.

We can contrast Ralph Touchett with another figure, a contemporary and nonfictional character: Lance Armstrong. As I write these lines in the late winter of 2013, Armstrong is offering a partial confession of his use of banned drugs to Oprah Winfrey. Up until 2012, the name Lance Armstrong stood for courage, commitment, and intensity. After being diagnosed with a metastasizing testicular cancer in 1996, he underwent aggressive chemotherapy. Throughout his ordeal, he maintained that he would race again. He was often nearly alone in this belief. His major sponsor dropped him, and he had trouble finding a team with which to race in top-level competition. Eventually, he was picked up by the United States Postal Service team, and went on to win seven Tour de France titles. In addition, he supported cancer research through the Lance Armstrong Foundation for Cancer, later known by its more popular name LiveStrong, recognized around the country through the ubiquitous yellow bracelets that were sold for fundraising.

During much of his rise to the top of the racing world, he was dogged by charges of illegal doping. He vigorously denied these charges and often threatened legal action against those who made them. In one case, he sued the publisher of a French exposé on his doping (*L.A. Confidentiel: les secrets de Lance Armstrong*), one of their major sources (his masseuse Emma O'Reilly) as well as the UK newspaper the *Sunday Times*, which referred to the book. The latter case was settled for a tidy sum, and is now the subject of a countersuit by the *Times*. Over the course of the summer of 2012, Armstrong's denials lost what might have remained of their plausibility, culminating in the US Anti-Doping Agency's stripping him of his seven Tour titles.

For many, Lance Armstrong evokes ambivalent feelings, perhaps even contradictory ones. His struggle against cancer and his determination to overcome obstacles as well as his contribution to cancer research remain a powerful draw to those who have admired him. However, recent months have seen the emergence of a darker side to these same qualities. The US Anti-Doping Agency has accused him of running one of the most pervasive and sophisticated doping operations in sports history. He is alleged to have been ruthless to anyone who opposed him. It is as though the same qualities that drove him to overcome cancer and ascend to the top of the cycling world were in evidence in his desire to win at any cost and to destroy those who sought to bar the way.

In one sense, Ralph Touchett and Lance Armstrong are kin. Both of their lives express the narrative value of steadfast commitment. To be sure, they express them in very different ways. Touchett's commitment is to those for whom he cares. (He treats others kindly, but without the quiet determination to look after their well-being that characterizes his relationship with his father and Isabel.) Armstrong's commitment is to winning. Nevertheless, both of them are exemplars of determined perseverance.

In two other ways, however, they seem very different. First, Ralph Touchett is someone who elicits our moral approval. Like many characters in Henry James's fiction, he is complex and flawed, that is to say that he is human. It is hard to read *The Portrait of a Lady*, however, without being moved by his dedication to his father and to Isabel as well as his general amiability with anyone who crosses his path. His visit to Rome as he is dying is undertaken with an enviable subtlety: he does not impose on Isabel's household, where he would be unwelcome to her husband. Instead, he parks himself in a local hotel and through a mutual friend allows Isabel to discover he is there. Most of us would like to have at least one friend like him, and in any case the real world would seem a little better off if it actually contained a Ralph Touchett.

Lance Armstrong's life, by contrast, has been revealed, or at least universally portrayed, as an example of how not to treat others. His demand for unwavering loyalty and his alleged brutality to those who refused to offer it is stunning in its callousness. It stands in starkest contrast to Ralph Touchett's sensitivity. Even his recent confession of doping to Oprah Winfrey appeared to many to be a cynical attempt to revive his reputation and allow him to participate again in competitive events. His regard for others seems to lie at the opposite moral pole from Touchett's.

The other contrast between the two is a bit speculative, at least as concerns Armstrong's life. Ralph Touchett, as we have seen, is not a happy man. He keeps his emotions at a safe distance. He is never entirely present to himself or engaged with others. His life does not display the attunement, engagement, or endorsement that Haybron offers us as the elements of happiness. This is not because he is depressed or miserable. Even those conditions would require a closer mesh between his emotions and his living. Rather, it is because he is not wholly an inhabitant of his own life.

Lance Armstrong, at least as I imagine him, displays a very different relation to his life. He seems entirely present to it. Before he was caught out, I suspect that he was happy in much the way Haybron describes. Perhaps he was not as attuned as one who was less driven would be. Since he was so ruthless to those who opposed him, it is not difficult to imagine that he saw the world as more potentially hostile than that element of happiness would allow. However, his intense focus allowed him, probably more than most of us, to experience the vital flow associated with engagement. And, as long as the world was cooperating with him, as it did for many years, it is likely that he affirmed his life in the way characteristic of endorsement. Moreover, since Haybron sees engagement and endorsement as largely built on attunement, we can at least speculate that there was enough of a tranquil relation to the world to allow the other two to emerge. And even if my speculations overstate the case here, it is certainly true that Armstrong was more tethered to his life than Ralph Touchett was to his.

How do we feel about these two different lives? In both cases, there is an ambivalence at play for many of us. This ambivalence would stem from a different source for Armstrong than for Touchett. At a first go, we might say that while Armstrong's life seems to be meaningful in the way we have discussed, at least up until 2012, it is less than morally adequate; while Touchett's life, though morally adequate, is deficient on the side of meaning. Armstrong's life is a bit like Hendrix's life, although more deeply morally compromised. Both lives expressed intensity and a steadfast commitment to their respective projects of cycling and music. And both may have left bodies in their wake, although in Hendrix's case those bodies are more a by-product of his intensity while in Armstrong's it was a necessity to keep the project viable. Many of us admire Armstrong and Hendrix in one way, and are uncomfortable—or in Armstrong's case, even repelled—by them in another.

Reflecting on Armstrong's life will lead us directly into the vexed relation between meaning and morality. Before turning there, I would like to linger a bit over Touchett's life. It, too, displays a complicated relation between meaning and morality, but in a less perplexing way. Touchett's life is moral, but is impoverished in its meaningfulness. This is not because it lacks narrative value. Like Armstrong, Touchett is steadfast. What is missing is not what Wolf would call objective attractiveness but instead subjective attraction. There is a hollowness that haunts Touchett's life. It is the hollowness that makes him unhappy. He is not void of emotion. Touchett is hardly a shell of a human being. His emotional connection to his father and to Isabel is palpable. The problem is subtler. His irony and humor keep him from being entirely bound to his own desires, desires whose satisfaction he feels he doesn't entirely deserve. It is as though he stands at a slight distance from himself, not altogether approving of what he sees. He cannot really endorse his life. His humor is a way of fostering distance between himself and his emotions, ensuring that he is never aligned with what he would want for himself.

If a meaningful life is one where "subjective attraction meets objective attractiveness," Touchett's life is impoverished with regard to meaningfulness because it is depleted, although not entirely destitute, of subjective attraction. To be sure, he is attracted to others, most notably Isabel Archer and his father. But he cannot allow himself to inhabit his attraction without holding himself in reserve. Although he is moral and displays at least one narrative value associated with meaningfulness, his life is wanting in meaningfulness because of this disallowance.

One might want to ask why there is a need for subjective attraction in order for there to be meaningfulness. Why is Touchett's life lacking in meaningfulness? Perhaps he is not entirely engaged with his life. Nevertheless, he contributes to the lives of those around him. While he is not happy, neither is he miserable. The world of *The Portrait of a Lady* is better for his existence in it. In our second chapter, we saw that for Wolf a life can be a good one without being entirely meaningful. One could live a morally valuable life and yet still be alienated from it in a way that saps its meaningfulness. As she put it, "If one usually finds her daily activities boring, if she typically feels alienated from the roles and projects she is nonetheless bound to occupy and pursue, if she is inclined to describe herself as feeling empty or even dead inside as she goes through the motions of her life, then that life is less than satisfactorily meaningful." Touchett, of course, would not be inclined to describe himself as empty or dead inside, first because that would be going too far in his case and second because that would be a more serious self-description than he would allow.

Even so, why should emptiness or alienation be a bar to meaningfulness?

In the case of a person who is moral without being alienated, there is likely to be little difficulty in seeing their life as meaningful. And most moral lives involve a set of commitments that express narrative values like courage or steadfastness or personal integrity or what Aristotle calls patience or mildness or good temper—an evenness of spirit that he contrasts with irascibility on the one hand and emotional vacancy on the other. That is to say, where a person is engaged with her life and is living morally, the meaningful and the moral will likely coincide. It is when they diverge, either through immorality (the Armstrong case) or disengagement (Ralph Touchett) that the question arises. For the moment, it is the latter question, whether an alienated but moral life can be meaningful, that concerns us.

Before proceeding any further, I should note that little has been said about what constitutes a moral life. I have assumed that, between those of you reading this book and me, there is some broad agreement on certain intuitions about moral rightness and wrongness. For instance, I haven't argued that Lance Armstrong's callous treatment of those who crossed him was actually morally wrong, but have instead hoped it would be taken for granted. I will continue to do so. I would dearly love to offer my view of the nature of morality as well as the character of meaningfulness. But that would take not only another book but several more. And frankly there are a lot of philosophers who are better able to tell that story than I am. For our purposes, relying on some uncontroversial moral intuitions should suffice.

Given that caveat, we remain faced with the question of

whether a life can lack subjective attraction and still be meaningful. In addressing this question, we must bear in mind that with regard to meaningfulness we are almost always within the realm of the more and the less. This is particularly true when it comes to subjective attraction. It is difficult to imagine someone who lacks all subjective attraction except perhaps if he is severely depressed or even comatose. So we might reformulate the question as one of whether a lack of subjective attraction diminishes the meaningfulness of a life. Does Touchett's life lose meaningfulness because he maintains distance from his deepest emotions?

It does. Touchett is not entirely in touch with his own life. There is a sense in which his life is not *here*, where he is living it, but *over there*, where he observes it while keeping it at arm's length. He does not wholeheartedly inhabit his own life. He participates in a life in which his life is not really his. Of course, in an obvious way it is his life. Whose life would it be if not his? But in another way, it isn't. He occupies his life like an ill-fitting set of clothes. It doesn't mold to him neatly, but rather hangs loosely from his soul. The point of his particular brand of humor is to ensure that his life does not get too close to him. And in that sense, he is distant from the meaningfulness his life might have for him.

Ralph Touchett exhibits the narrative value of steadfastness. But he does not allow himself to align his emotions with that exhibition. This lack of alignment not only contributes to his being unhappy; it also diminishes the fit between himself and the narrative value he displays. Because of this, we can say that there is a loss of meaningfulness.

Something goes missing in Touchett's life. What goes missing is not in his moral commitments, which are unimpeachable. The absence lies somewhere else. It is in the detachment that prevents him from altogether inhabiting himself. That is why we might admire him for his goodness while not wanting to hold him up as a model of living. And it is because of this that we would say that his life, while hardly meaningless, is impoverished in its meaningfulness. His depleted capacity for subjective attraction drains meaningfulness from his life.

To be subjectively attracted to one's life does not require that one be satisfied with it in an unequivocal way. It demands rather that one be involved with it, engaged by it. Susan Wolf's book *Meaning in Life and Why It Matters* contains commentaries by other intellectuals that follow her discussion. One of them is by the philosopher Robert Adams, who recalls the life of Claus von Stauffenberg. Stauffenberg was a German officer during World War II, although he despised the Nazi regime. Along with several others, he sought to save Germany from the scourge of Hitler's reign, and in the summer of 1944 led the famous Operation Valkyrie, a failed attempt to assassinate Hitler. Afterward, he was shot by the Nazi regime. Adams comments that Stauffenberg found his life and his projects, even the failed project to kill Hitler, to be meaningful. But, he wonders, "suppose he did not. More precisely, suppose that in the moment of failure he was so disappointed and so depressed that he thought his life was meaningless. Should we in that case conclude that it was in fact meaningless? I think that conclusion would be implausible."[32]

I agree with Adams that it would be implausible to conclude that Stauffenberg's life would have lacked meaning even if he were to think so at the end of it. Meaning is not just about, as he puts it, "feeling good."[33] What would make Stauffenberg's life meaningful from the subjective side would be his wholehearted ratification of what he was doing *while he was doing it*, his sense that he was engaged in something important, something that reflected who he thought he should be. The fact that he might have looked back upon his life with a sense of regret or failure would not detract from the existence of the engagement in his life while he was living through it.

If subjective attraction need not require that one feel good or entirely satisfied with one's life, either during its unfolding or looking back at it retrospectively, then perhaps Haybron's sense of attunement is not as important to meaningfulness as it is to happiness. Recall that for Haybron, the tranquility of attunement is the basis on which the flow of engagement and the ratification of endorsement are founded. Together they amount to the "psychic affirmation" of one's life. We saw that with Lance Armstrong, and can see again with Claus von Stauffenberg, that there can be deep engagement within the context of a world that seems hostile. This might lead us to think that there can be engagement and endorsement without attunement, or, in the end, subjective attraction without happiness. Perhaps the subjective attraction required for meaningfulness is just very different from the kind of happiness Haybron has in mind.

We are in danger of moving too quickly here. I have spoken of subjective attraction as being akin to the happiness Haybron has described for us. To be sure, it need not be the same thing—although in some cases it is, as when a dedicated parent or someone brought alive by adventure gets to spend large parts of their life raising their kids or braving new challenges in uninhibited ways. However, even when subjective attraction does not coincide with happiness, it would be going too far to say that there is no place for attunement in subjective attraction. It would be more accurate to say that in cases like Stauffenberg's the attunement probably results from the engagement and endorsement rather than being the basis for them. Stauffenberg derived what tranquility he possessed from his comfort that what he was doing was what he should be doing. His attunement did not lead to his ability to be engaged with the world in a way that he ratified; instead, his dedication to the task of saving Germany from Hitler's devastation brought him whatever inner peace his conscience would allow.

If this is right, then we would not describe Stauffenberg as happy but would not say he is entirely unhappy either (except, in Adams's speculative rendering, at the end of his life). Rather, he was engaged with his life in a way that resembles happiness. It is hard to imagine how someone involved in resistance against the Nazis, particularly when one is German himself, could be considered happy. And yet there is something in the recognition of the righteousness of one's cause and the importance of seeking to see it through that is not entirely divorced from happiness either. Moreover, the aspect of oneself that is not entirely divorced from happiness is the subjective attraction that is the personal side of meaningfulness.

In discussing the fictional life of Ralph Touchett and the real life of Claus von Stauffenberg, we have been asking the question of whether subjective attraction is necessary for meaningfulness. The answer seems to be that it is. A moral life from which one is alienated is deficient in meaning. It rarely lacks all meaning, since, as we saw, very few lives are devoid of subjective attraction. But we can say this: the fact that a life is a moral one does not guarantee that it is a meaningful one. An alienated moral life would not be any more meaningful than an alienated nonmoral, or in some cases immoral, life.

But how about the other way around: can a life be meaning-ful without being moral? Here is where Lance Armstrong com-mands our attention. Speculating that Armstrong had subjec-tive attraction to his sport, and recognizing that he displayed the narrative value of steadfastness, we might say that his life was to that degree meaningful. However, given his treatment of many with whom he came into contact, we would hesi-tate to call it moral. If the allegations raised against him by his former mechanic, massage therapist, and others are true, we might well say that Armstrong's life was significantly im-moral. To call it evil would probably be a stretch, but it would be a stretch in the right direction.

Consider the classic image of the narcissistic rock star who sleeps with whatever groupies cross his path, trashes hotel rooms, periodically makes life miserable for his band mates, and has no filter for his moods or his mouth. He also throws himself into creating music and loses himself utterly in per-formances. When he is writing music he is absorbed in it and unerringly nasty to anyone who interrupts him. Onstage he is fueled by the audience, playing with abandon and occasion-ally throwing himself into the crowd, letting them push him along over top with their arms. (We imagine this person play-ing electric guitar, don't we? Not bass, not drums, nothing acoustic, and rarely a singer without an instrument. Always the electric guitar.)

In my generation, many if not most of us went through a period wanting to be rock stars. Initially it was the Beatles that inspired me. (My first vinyl album was *Meet the Beatles*.) In fact, there are pictures of me as a ten-year-old forcing my family to pose like a rock band with little cardboard electric guitars I had drawn. At that time I didn't think about the narcissistic part, and I was too young to consider the role that groupies generally play, but I wanted to be onstage in front of an audience with my guitar. That dream has not entirely left me. When I go to rock concerts, I still get the urge to buy a guitar and learn how to play. I know I am not alone among my peers in having had—and continuing to harbor—the occasional reverie of shredding in front of adoring crowds, although I don't go in for Jimi Hendrix's lighting his guitar on fire or even smashing it on the amplifiers at the end of a performance. Judging from the development of my own children and the popularity of *American Idol*, the seduction of this image, although with different icons, has not diminished.

Many of us admire rock stars for their lives, even at times to the point of envy. Suppose, though, we were to discover that one of the stars we admire is indeed as narcissistic as the stereotype I painted above. Would this eliminate our admiration or our view that his life is worthwhile, even if we reject the morally compromised elements of it? Would we shift our view from good and worthy life to bad and unworthy one? Hardly. To be sure, learning the moral downside of a rock star does not (I hope) increase admiration. Instead it leads to a sense of conflict. On the one hand, he is leading an interesting and even inspiring life. On the other hand, he's a jerk. Our feelings are at odds with themselves, often in ways that we seek to reconcile. We tell ourselves that he is probably not as depraved as the media make him out to be, or that these other aspects of his character are the necessary dark side to his creativity, or that everyone knows he is like this so it's not really doing any damage. But what attempts at reconciliation expose is that there are two discordant attitudes in play here, one that attracts us to him and another that pushes us away.

Chapter Four

In addition to Lance Armstrong or the image of the rock stars, we can find numerous examples of lives that elicit this kind of conflicted attitude. It is the intense lover who leaves bodies in his wake when the embers of his love begin to burn less brightly. It is the athlete whose focus and skill allow him to dominate a sport but who is so self-absorbed in his desire to win that those around him do not show up on his moral radar. (Some say that Michael Jordan and Kobe Bryant are like this.) It is the person who remains a steadfast friend to someone who is himself a morally dubious character. It is the witty writer who cannot pass up a good line even at the expense of others, perhaps best exemplified by the activity of the Algonquin Round Table in New York in the 1920s, one of whose members, Dorothy Parker, once commented that a performance by the great actress Katharine Hepburn "ran the gamut of emotions from A to B." These are people whose lives we are drawn to and repelled by at the same time.

If we were to be moralistic about this conflict, we would be ashamed that we feel an attraction to lives like these. We would seek to repress any admiration of such lives or any longing to emulate them. The allure of these lives would express not so much any worthy quality they possessed as our own moral deficiency.

But this kind of moralism is misplaced. It is a sad and constricted way to look at life. And because it is constricted is misses something important about lives like these, something that our feelings of conflict express, however inchoately. After all, the rock star is really committed to his music, the lover really intense in his passions, the Round Table members really subtle in their jaded perceptions, Armstrong really dedicated to racing. These are not insignificant details about these lives, and there is something commendable, perhaps at times even precious, about them.

They do not make the lives in which they are embedded more morally praiseworthy, and they do not cancel out the moral failures that attach to these lives. If they did, we would not feel conflicted about them. We would instead weigh the moral contribution these aspects of their lives made against the moral failures those lives exhibited and come up with a result. We would say either that these lives are, on balance, morally okay or that they were not.

But that is not how we feel. We feel conflicted precisely because there doesn't seem to be a single scale on which to weigh these aspects of their lives with their moral deficiencies. It is as though there were two scales, a moral one on which these lives come out poorly and another one on which they come out much better. Our eyes shift back and forth between these scales, not settling on one of them.

What is this other scale? It is that of meaningfulness, and especially the narrative values these lives express. Rather than a conflict between morally praiseworthy aspects of their lives and morally deficient ones, the conflict is between morality and meaningfulness.

To see this, reflect on the intense lover. To be an intense lover—in this case a serially intense lover—is not merely to have had an intense affair. An intense lover is not a flash in the pan. He (or she) is someone who is entirely absorbed in his passion, as long as it lasts. While it can be devastating to the beloved when the embers of that love begin to dim, the ecstasy of the time before that can rival the joys offered by a more committed but more pedestrian partner. But the intense lover moves on, offering himself entirely to another until, of course, the ardor once again fades. What draws us to the intense lover is not that he was once intense with one person, but that his intensity characterizes him. It is a central theme of his life. To him, love is not a matter of long-term companionship. It is instead a consuming desire for another, a desire whose fury is perhaps destined to subside, even if, in the throes of it, its end cannot be conceived. It is intensity as a narrative value, not as an episode, that lends this lover the peculiar appeal that he possesses.

It would be too much to say that we admire the intense lover. More accurately, we admire him—or long to be him, or perhaps just don't dismiss him—*in a certain way*. But in another way, he elicits our scorn. After all, there are the victims of a love that once seemed so promising and now has vanished. And, we might say, after a couple of these affairs he should have known better than to delve in again. He should have been more responsible. Our admiration (or longing, or at least reluctance to dismiss) contends with our moral censure.

In the end, for at least some of us, the censure wins out. The lover was wrong. He should be been more attentive to those upon whom he lavished his affection. The intensity should have given way to a more sober respect for the beloved. But even if that becomes our judgment, it is still not without remainder. The draw of intensity might be outweighed, but it is not cancelled. It lingers in the background, casting a shadow that is never entirely erased. The moral judgment might be our final one, but it is not our only one.

Our reflections on Ralph Touchett revealed that we might live a moral life without its being very meaningful. Now we can see the converse: a life can be meaningful without being moral. This does not require of us that we abstain from judging such a life and finding it wanting. It does not require that we refrain from intervening, from confronting the person whose life it is with their moral failures, or asking them to construct their lives differently. Meaningfulness is not a "Get Out of Jail Free" card. In some cases confrontation would seem to be the appropriate response. With Lance Armstrong this seems certainly to be the case. In other cases, say that of the rock star or the intense lover, we might want to allow a little moral latitude. Whether to intervene depends on a number of factors specific to the person and the situation: how much harm he is causing, how likely it is that change will take place, how much damage to the person's own life will come from a significant reorientation of his trajectory, and so on. The distinction between morality and meaningfulness does not paralyze moral action.

What it does instead is to remind us of the complexity of human life. For many of us, particularly philosophers like me, there is a desire for closure. We want to be able to tie things up neatly and present them without anything loose hanging off the sides. If something is wrong, it needs to be wrong, period. It cannot be wrong, but . . . Philosophers in particular like philosophical systems, where everything has its place. Often, even when we find a system to be mistaken, if it is well-constructed we call it flawed but beautiful. We are drawn to it in the way we long for our childhood when, through our retrospective ignorance, things seemed simple.

Philosophers are not alone in this. For a person's judgment to have remainders, to have to say, "It is wrong, but . . ." is often uncomfortable. It reminds the one judging that there is more going on than that judgment can capture. It saps the righteousness from the verdicts we pronounce to ourselves or others. It is difficult to see lives, one's own life or that of others, as having other sides or of being able to be seen from other perspectives.

When I was a student of psychology before moving to philosophy, I had a teacher who said that the task of therapy was the difficult one of getting the client to recognize that there were other people in the world. Of course he didn't mean that clients in therapy don't recognize the existence of other human beings. Therapy clients aren't solipsists. The idea is that the way one sees the world is not the only way it can be seen, and people who see it differently are not necessarily wrong just because they do see it differently. For the client, at least in this teacher's eyes, the existence of other ways of seeing and taking up the world is an affront that needs to be expunged rather than a lesson on the limits of one's own vision. That is what therapy is supposed to change.

I don't know whether that view of therapy is any good; I left the field before I could find out. But as a life lesson, it has resonance. And one of the places it has resonance is in recognizing that human lives are more complex affairs than can be captured in moral judgment. Many of us would prefer the seamlessness of the moral and the meaningful. We would like them to blend together at both ends. That is, we would prefer a moral life automatically to be a meaningful one and an immoral life to be meaningless. But if meaningfulness is tied to narrative values, we must abandon this desire. We must instead take the conflicted feelings we have toward certain lives not as symptoms of our own moral lapses or as indicators that we have yet to arrive at a final judgment, but instead as accurate reflections of the irreducibility of human life to single measures.

Reflecting on this, we should not be surprised. After all, in a globalized world, where we recognize that even moral values can vary markedly across cultures, there seems no reason to deny that there can be conflict within a culture between different kinds of values. In thinking about our values, the goal is not to introduce an artificial simplicity. It is instead to grasp the complexity in the right way. Aristotle (of course, Aristotle) once said that "the educated person seeks exactness in each area to the extent that the nature of the subject allows."[34] One of the lessons of our reflecting on life's meaningfulness should be to affirm Aristotle's insight.

If moral lives need not be meaningful, and meaningful lives need not be moral, does that mean that the two sets of values are entirely divorced? That no amount of morality contributes to meaningfulness and no amount of immorality saps it? Things are more complicated and a bit more puzzling than this. On the one hand morality is no guarantee of meaning. Even where moral values converge with narrative ones— for example, in courage—there may still be the lack of subjective engagement that meaningfulness requires. Adding more courage will not fill this gap. Someone who consistently exhibits courage but in doing so feels that she is just going through the motions would be like Ralph Touchett: good but impoverished in meaning. It is likely that most people who dedicate themselves to living morally, however that is defined, are engrossed in that dedication. However, it need not be the case. There are people whose morality acts upon them not as a magnet but as a weight, a burden that they can neither embrace nor abandon.

On the other hand, however, I suspect that most of us would balk at saying that immorality can never sap meaningfulness. To see this, let's compare two imagined people participating in a deeply evil project, whether they are Nazis during World War II or soldiers during Pol Pot's regime in Cambodia or Hutus during the massacre of Tutsis in Rwanda in 1994. One soldier is dedicated to the evil project. He is a Nazi who believes the Jews must be exterminated or a Khmer Rouge who has a fiery hatred of intellectuals or a Hutu who can hardly be held back from using his machete on Tutu children. This person is steadfast in his commitment to the evil project and certainly subjectively engaged by it. And let's imagine that even after the evil project fails, he does not abandon his commitment to it. He lives in the hope that it will rise again. We know that there have been Nazis like this, and likely there are Khmer Rouge and Hutus who would qualify.

This person is living meaningfully by the standards for which I have argued. Subjective attraction has met a narrative value.

Compare him with a more reluctant participant, someone who feels compelled to engage in the evil—whether through coercion or a sense of loyalty to his people or moral uncertainty about what is right—but remains skeptical about what she is doing. She understands the reasons offered for the project, but something just seems wrong about it. She participates, but without feeling engaged. She kills fewer people than she might and lives afterward with regret over what she did. Perhaps she seeks to make amends in one way or another by visiting bereaved families or contributing to rebuilding their communities. Her life after the evil project is not devastated, but she is haunted by her participation. She should have listened to that nagging voice inside her when it would have made a difference.

By the criteria for meaningfulness I have proposed, her life would be less meaningful, at least in regard to the evil project, than that of the enthusiastic supporter of evil. She is never subjectively attracted by the project, and she displays no particular narrative values in regard to her participation. She does not even have the courage of refusal. But do we want to say that the life of the person committed to evil is more meaningful than her life?

I am reluctant to do so. It seems to me that while her life is not terribly meaningful—at least as far as the evil project plays a role in it—his life is even less so. His commitment to evil seems not to add to but rather subtract from its meaningfulness. However, this is the opposite of what one would expect based on the standards for meaningfulness I have laid out. For him, subjective attraction has indeed met objective attractiveness in the form of a narrative value, one that he sustains throughout his life. By contrast, her life would seem less meaningful from both the subjective and the objective sides.

How can this be accounted for?

There is, I think, a deep but elusive truth this example reveals. We might call it the asymmetrical relationship of morality and meaningfulness. While morality cannot add to meaningfulness, a severe immorality—what I have called *evil*—can subtract from it. Evil bends narrative values away from meaningfulness. Steadfastness and intensity are always admirable when they are oriented toward morally worthy projects. They cause us ambivalence when they lend meaning to a life that is not entirely moral. But when they are pressed into the service of evil, they actually detract from meaning. It is as though, when the person exhibiting those narrative values is engaged in something deeply immoral, narrative values shift their valence from supporting to undermining meaning.

One might think that this shift does not take place with all narrative values. For instance, if someone is courageous but still evil, doesn't our ambivalence about them remain? Here we might think of some suicide bombers who give their lives for a cause they have long been committed to but in doing so create evil. It might even be that the cause to which they are committed is itself evil. To be sure, not everyone would call a suicide bomber courageous. Fair enough. But let's leave that worry aside and ask: if a suicide bomber in the service of an evil cause could be considered courageous, would we have an example of someone whose narrative value still added meaningfulness to his life rather than detracting from it?

The answer to this question may be that it does, but only because courage, like other Aristotelian values, is a special case. Courage is not only a narrative value; it is also a moral one. Courage in a life plays two roles. It makes a life morally admirable and gives it a narrative theme that contributes meaning. When we admire courage in someone whose life is dedicated to evil, I suspect it is the residue of the moral value we are admiring, not the narrative value. The willingness to die for a cause is a quality we respect—if indeed we do in such cases—not because it lends a positive thematic unity to a life but because it displays a personal characteristic we associate with moral goodness. The difference between a courageous person committed to evil and a steadfast one lies in the former's possession of a moral quality that is lacking in the latter.

It seems, then, that narrative values (unless they possess a moral side) actually detract from meaningfulness when they are in the service of evil. Why is this, especially since in other cases they contribute to meaning? What causes this change of valence to occur?

In order for a life to be considered a meaningful one at all, it has to be a life that is in some way worth living. The worthiness of a life to be lived is a baseline quality. It allows meaningfulness to get off the ground. Some lives—evil ones—do not seem to fulfill that basic requirement. Those lives are not worth living on any accounting. And if they're not worth living on any accounting, then narrative values will not lend them meaningfulness.

In saying this, I am not saying that the person who is living the evil life is herself worthless. To say that would imply that it would be fine to kill her. It is the life she is living that is without worth. Her life is a waste, and in many ways worse than a waste. But it might still be the case that respect for her as a human being requires that, while we treat her life as worthless, we do not treat her person that way. In any event, that is a matter for moral reflection rather than the reflection on meaning that is our concern.

We are beginning to see our way to an answer to our question, but we have not arrived yet. If a life has to be worthwhile in some sense in order for it to be meaningful, this would explain why narrative values would not lend meaning to an evil life. But that is not enough to explain why they in fact seem often to *detract* from the meaningfulness of a life. It is not just that if a life cannot be taken as worthwhile in some basic way, then narrative values become irrelevant. They actually seem to work in the opposite direction, sapping meaning from a life. The lives of the committed Nazi and Khmer Rouge and Hutu murderer seem to many of us to be *less* meaningful than that of the more ambivalent participant. To account for this we need to say more.

In these cases, what the expression of narrative values of steadfastness or intensity accomplishes is to bind the person more closely to the evil. They increase the evil in two ways. First, they make it more likely that the person himself will commit evil acts. Second, they are ways in which the person associates himself with the evil, takes it on as part of his identity. Someone who identifies with Nazism or the genocide of the Khmer Rouge is certainly living a worse life than someone who does not. Steadfastness to either of these projects changes the valence of a narrative value because it presses toward the evil rather than moving away from it or at least being neutral with respect to it.

What holds for steadfastness and intensity would also hold for other narrative values. Someone who is subtle in her commitment to evil or intellectually curious in regard to it (think here of Josef Mengele and the notorious medical experiments on Jews that he performed) expresses a theme that augments rather than mitigates the ills stemming from that evil. If involvement with evil drains meaningfulness from a life, narrative values will be complicit in that draining by bringing the person displaying them closer to it in one way or another. In this way, narrative values change their valence from adding meaning to subtracting it when they partner with evil.

The relation of narrative values to moral values, then, is a complex and asymmetrical one. While morality cannot add to meaningfulness, a profound immorality—real evil—can detract from it. Moreover, narrative values, in alliance with that profound immorality, can deplete meaningfulness rather than adding to it. Morality and meaning, while distinct realms of value, intersect and affect each other in the expression of a life.

If narrative values are not simply a type of moral value, can we consider them instead as a type of aesthetic value? Might we say that narrative values, although they do not make lives morally better, make them more artistic in some way or another?

Recall here the words of Michel Foucault from the previous chapter: "What strikes me is the fact that in our society, art has become something which is related only to objects and not to individuals, or to life. That art is something which is specialized or which is done by experts who are artists. But couldn't everyone's life become a work of art? Why should the lamp or the house be an art object, but not our life?" We might reframe Foucault's question in a somewhat similar way (one that admittedly runs roughshod over debates about the nature of art) by asking whether a life can be beautiful, in addition to interesting, and so forth, in the ways we have already discussed.

There are, of course, diverse ways an art object can be beautiful. And those ways depend in part on what that object is. What makes for a beautiful painting? There are several possibilities. Van Gogh's paintings, with their striking and expressive colors, are beautiful to many people. When I look at one, I am gripped, almost hypnotized. It is as though the colors reach out and draw me toward them. *Starry Night* (or the less well known *Starry Night over the Rhone*, of which we have a print in our living room) is an invitation, or even a demand, to stand slightly chilled under the midnight sky and wonder at the vibrant harmony of the cosmos.

By contrast, a painting by the American Mark Rothko works very differently. His most famous works have been labeled Color Field paintings. They are large paintings with several distinct areas of color. For instance, in *No. 61 (Rust and Blue)* there is a deep red on the top third of the painting, a lighter blue in the middle, and a bluish purple at the bottom, surrounded by a border of a middle shade of blue. The size of the paintings has the effect, like Van Gogh's, of drawing in the spectator. The experience, though, is one of peacefulness rather than animation. When I sit in front of a Rothko, my mood becomes meditative. The stillness rather than the energy of the world comes to the fore.

What elicits these distinct reactions, rendering both of them beautiful in their different ways? It lies primarily in the colors and their placement on the canvas. Van Gogh arranges them in contrasting ways, while Rothko in more harmonious ones. Van Gogh uses more primary colors, Rothko mixed ones. Van Gogh lays paint on thickly, so that the colors reach out from the canvas, while Rothko's paint rests flat and serene within its borders. But for both of them, it is what is happening on the canvas through the way the colors appear (and the way the paint is laid on) in themselves and in relation to one another that creates the beauty we experience.

We might be tempted to relate some of the themes of painting to those of narrative values. After all, isn't the vibrancy of a Van Gogh like the narrative value of intensity? And might we not think of serenity as a narrative value? Imagining a life characterized by the understated spirituality of some of Rothko's finer paintings would seem to offer another theme that could characterize a life in a meaningful way. If this is right, couldn't we assimilate in some way narrative values to the aesthetic values characteristic of an art like painting?

This is a temptation we should resist. It is not that there is nothing in common between the values of these paintings and narrative values. But a quick assimilation would miss a crucial element of narrative values. A painting does not unfold over time. To be sure, the creation of a painting takes time. The painting itself, though, when it is complete, is all there and of a piece. Its beauty, whether harmonious or vibrant or something else, occurs in the contemporaneous relations of its elements. The values expressed by a painting are synchronic: they exist in the same time and place. Lives, by contrast, are diachronic. They unfold over time. Narrative values concern lives in their chronological unfolding rather than in a particular moment of time. In fact, it is hard to imagine how a life could ever be synchronic the way a painting is. We are always moving in time, never all of a piece except at death. Even when we view a painting, although the painting itself is static before us, our eyes range over it in a chronological way.

The intensity of color contrasts in a Van Gogh painting is different from a life of narrative intensity. It is an intensity that arises from the synchronic relation of colors. Even the intensity that *I* feel when I gaze at *Starry Night* is different from a narrative value. It is a subjective attraction rather than the objective attractiveness captured by the narrative value of intensity. While the two types of intensity are not utterly distinct— they are both, after all, intense—they are different ways of being intense. To assimilate narrative values to the aesthetic values which characterize painting would neglect the chronological character of lives that is the foundation of narrative values.

Perhaps then a diachronic art like music would offer a more promising arena of convergence. Like human life and unlike painting or sculpture, music unfolds over time. Could it be that narrative values have an affinity with musical ones?

Many of the values associated with music seem to have no

correlate or analogy among the narrative values. Melodiousness and rhythm are difficult to cast as narrative values. What would a melodious or rhythmic life look like? Even a value like harmony would be difficult to press into service in describing a human life. What would it mean to say that a human life is harmonious? One might, I suppose, mean that the different aspects or activities of that life fit together in complementary ways. That would certainly be a positive thing to say about a life, but it is not clearly a narrative value. It is a theme that characterizes not how someone goes about living, but instead how the different ways one goes about living resonate with one another. A harmonious life, rather than being like a courageous or subtle life or a life of personal integrity, would be a life in which these (or other) narrative values blended together in a proper balance. If harmony is a value, then, it is not a narrative value but instead what we might call a metanarrative value, a value about the way in which narrative values interact in a particular life. If this is right, then harmony might be among another set of values that lend meaningfulness to our living. But even if it is, it is not among the narrative values.

The difficulty in seeking to assimilate narrative values to musical ones is that while musical values concern sounds, narrative values concern living. Even though sounds occur in the world and engage with other elements in that world (for instance they travel through the air, bouncing off certain surfaces and becoming muffled in others), they don't engage in the way of human action. We live through our engagement with the world, taking it up in certain ways and letting it go in others. Our action is responsive to what is happening in the world in complex ways that audio waves are not. The narrative values that human lives express are based upon those complex engagements with the world. And so while we might not be capable of simple diachronic expressions like melody or rhythm, sounds are not capable of complex themes like intellectual curiosity or steadfastness.

A final candidate for narrative values might seem, at first glance, to be the most obvious one: literature. Since much of literature is narrative, could narrative values be assimilated to values associated with literature? After all, we have had recourse to a number of fictional characters over the course of this book, from Faulkner's Dilsey to Calvino's Marco Polo to James's Ralph Touchett. Might it be that what makes life meaningful is that it can express the types of value characteristic of literature (or, in the same vein, movies)?

Even this attempt at assimilation would be fraught. To see why, we need to distinguish the characters in literature from the literature itself. The value we associated with Dilsey was steadfastness. That is not the value we might attach to *The Sound and the Fury* as a literary creation. There are many positive things one might say about the novel. It peers deeply into the human soul. It captures some of the most wrenching conflicts in Southern life. Its treatment of many of the central characters is poignant. But it is not steadfast in the way someone's living might be steadfast.

Perhaps, though, it is intense. Might we say that *The Sound and the Fury* is intense, and that, in contrast to *Starry Night*, its intensity is not all there of a piece but instead unfolds over time? Its intensity lies instead in the time of reading it, in the unfolding of the words as one turns the pages.

What is it to say of a novel that it is intense?

One way to think of it would be to say that it elicits intensity in the reader. Each time I read *The Sound and the Fury* I am indeed mesmerized by the prose. To look at it this way would be to say that the quality of Faulkner's writing of being at once gripping and hypnotic is something that it elicits in the reader. It would be a matter of subjective attraction. The novel is not intense in what it does; it is intense in what it does to me. This is different from a narrative value. It lies on the subjective side of meaningfulness rather than the objective side.

But there is another way to look at the novel's intensity that brings it closer to narrative values. We might say that the intensity of *The Sounds and the Fury* is *expressed* in the unfolding of its words just as the intensity of living is *expressed* in its actions. Although readers may feel intense while reading it, that is not where the real intensity lies. It lies rather in the novel itself, just as the intensity of a narrative value lies in the living itself. Would this way of seeing things not bring narrative values closer to literary ones?

If we think that artistic values arise only in the experience the audience has of an art object, then we will see the values of literature as involving only subjective attraction in the sense Wolf discussed and that we saw in the second chapter. But if we think that art objects can be valuable in themselves, then literary values take on an objective attractiveness and in that way come closer to narrative values. We cannot resolve this debate here. It is as old as the philosophy of art itself. But suppose we chose the second alternative. Suppose we thought that literary values were indeed objective. Would that bring the diachronic values associated with literature (or perhaps film) in league with narrative values? More pointedly, would narrative values be a species of literary ones? Or are literary values, like musical ones, too distant from our living to be considered candidates for narrative values?

Narrative values are themes expressed in a person's living. One looks at the activities of a life and the way someone participates in those activities in order to discern whether a particular narrative value is expressed. With novels, one looks at the words on the page and how those words unfold in order to see what particular literary value is expressed. Say in both cases we find intensity. *The Sound and the Fury* is intense and Jimi Hendrix's life was intense. Are they both intense in a similar enough way to say that the narrative value is the same thing as the literary one? Alternatively put, might Hendrix's life be taken as a text, expressing intensity as a literary text would?

For my own part, I would like to resist the idea. I have no strong argument for this, and I can accept that there might be overlap between narrative and literary values. But it seems to me that actions, while they can be analogized to the unfolding of words, cannot be reduced to them. Just as painting concerns colors and music concerns sounds and literature concerns words, narrative values concern the doings of living. To be sure, all of these values are matters of the *how*. Narrative values concern the how of living; painterly, musical, and literary values concern the how of colors and sounds and words. But while one lives among colors and sounds and words, living itself is distinct from them. Its values, it seems to me, constitute their own realm.

In this way, narrative values are more like moral values than aesthetic ones. Morality concerns our living. It tells us ways in which we should or should not go about it and draws lines between what is permissible and what is not. It concerns our acts or the trajectory of our lives. It tells us what we ought to do or how we ought to develop ourselves. Narrative values, while they are not matters of *should* or *ought* in the same way moral values are, are focused on living in ways that will make life more valuable in a particular way—the way of meaningfulness.

But since narrative values do not concern what we should or ought to do, they also share something with aesthetic values. They are like them in the sense of lending life something very much like beauty. We do not say that an artist is obliged to create a beautiful work of art in the way we say that someone is obliged to treat human beings with a degree of respect. But we are gratified when she does so. Just the same, a meaningful life—in contrast to a morally decent one—is not something one is obliged to live. It adds something to a life when it expresses one or several narrative values, but a life that is impoverished in narrative values is not derelict in the way that a life impoverished in morality would be. Of course a meaningful life not only adds something to the world; it also adds something to the experience of the person living it. But just so, an artistic creation adds something to the artist. It makes (or often makes) her life better alongside its offering the world an object of significance. An art object, like a meaningful life, adds a certain beauty to the world and a certain significance to the person living it. It is nobody's obligation to live meaningfully, but something worthwhile is created when someone does, something that answers to Michel Foucault's question about thinking of life as art.

Narrative values may not be reducible to any of the values we associate with particular arts: painting and sculpture, music, or perhaps even literary values. However, they do seem to form a set of something like aesthetic values for considering our own lives or those of others. While we may be hesitant to say that a meaningful life is a beautiful life, and while on the other hand there is also a hesitance to say that aesthetic values must concern the beautiful, the significance meaningfulness lends to a life seems to align it more deeply to aesthetics than to morality. As we have seen, morality and meaning have a vexed relationship.

Having come this far, there is a question that remains, and it is perhaps the most difficult one. We have isolated a set of values, narrative values, that I have said constitute the objective side (or at least one objective side) of meaningfulness. If our lives are to be meaningful, then they must not only feel meaningful to us; they must also express a meaning that is not simply a matter of personal taste. They must have a worth that is grounded in something outside what you or I happen to enjoy or admire.

But what is it for a narrative value to be objective?

This is not simply a philosophical worry. It is a worry that arose for us in discussing meaning in the first chapter. There I said that we are no longer attracted to Aristotle's assumption that the universe offers a telos of meaning for human lives to embody. I also denied that God could ground meaningfulness. Why should we accept that narrative values are any better grounded than Aristotle's telos or God's pronouncements? What gives them their force? If narrative values are to supply what previous accounts of meaning have lacked, then how do they avoid the difficulties faced by those earlier accounts?

Without an answer to this question, appealing to narrative values as a way to give meaning to life would only be another form of what Camus calls philosophical suicide. It is, then, to that difficult and elusive task that we now turn.

Chapter Four

Chapter Five

JUSTIFYING OURSELVES
TO OURSELVES

Our lives gain meaningfulness when we are engaged in a life trajectory that expresses one or more narrative values. When we are absorbed by the unfolding of our life, when it makes sense to us to continue to do what we do, when we endorse our projects: that is half of it. When that unfolding occurs by way of subtlety or integrity or intellectual curiosity or intensity or any other positive value that would capture its temporal character, then we have the other half of it. To the extent that these two halves meet, we have a meaningful life.

Or so I have argued.

But a piece of the puzzle is missing. It is the most difficult piece. It is the one we were confronted with at the outset.

Why should we consider such a life meaningful? In particular, why should we think that narrative values can offer some kind of objective measure of meaningfulness that Aristotle's *telos* or God's pronouncements could not? If neither of these were capable of grounding meaning, why would narrative values do so? What makes them something more than another example of what Camus would call philosophical suicide?

Answering this question will take us through the most difficult terrain of this philosophical journey. It requires us to confront the question of how to ground narrative values, of how to give reasons for thinking that they exist independently of what any particular person, or even any group of people, thinks about them. It requires us to answer the question of why narrative values are not arbitrary, but instead are rooted in something firm.

What is at stake here is what philosophers call the problem of objectivity. What makes something objective? In particular, what makes narrative values objective? I have called them the objective side of meaningfulness. How might we be justified in thinking of them as objective?

Some people think that only science gives us objectivity. It does so because it is rooted in the material world. When I say that water has the chemical structure H2O, this is an objective statement because there is water out there that we can test to back it up. Even a scientific view more distant from immediate reality can be substantiated by the material world. Take a theory like evolution by natural selection, for instance. We can test that theory by what it predicts we would find in the fossil record, in the particular spread of life around the planet, and in the genetic structures of living beings. In fact, when we test that theory we find it well substantiated. It seems to be objectively grounded.

Of course, scientific theories can survive a good bit of contrary evidence. Ptolemaic theory, which posited that all celestial objects revolve around the earth, lasted for hundreds of years in the face of some pretty obvious evidence that the planets and stars were not fulfilling their roles of obedient revolution. All of this was accounted for in strange ways, for instance by claims about epicycles—celestial objects moving closer or further away from the earth during their revolutions by means of other revolutions. Nevertheless, eventually the weight of the evidence became overwhelming and Ptolemy's geocentric view was supplanted by a heliocentric one, and then by more sophisticated views. This happened because there is a material world that can confirm or reject the claims that were made about it. That material world is what guarantees (or at least frames) the objectivity of science.

When it comes to values, narrative or otherwise, there is no material world to confirm or disconfirm them. If we want to know what water is and whether there is any, we look around. If we want to know what steadfastness is and whether there is any, where could we look? We talk as though there is goodness or badness in the world or in people's actions, but how could we justify that? What might back up the claim that torture is wrong or that an intense life is valuable? For that matter, what might show those claims to be mistaken? When we seek objectivity for values, we seem adrift.

Values are things we make up. We decide that torture is wrong or that intensity is good or that beauty is an important element of art. We don't discover it, or if we do, it is not because it is part of the given character of the universe. Rather, it is because we have been taught to find it there. We may be revolted by cruelty, and that revulsion may be part of our human character. But we condemn cruelty *as wrong* because we have been initiated into a moral practice in which rightness and wrongness are ascribed to the cruelty. We could never discover it in the world in the way we could discover the existence of water. And if we couldn't discover it directly, we could never have evidence for its being there in the way we have evidence for electrons or evolution by natural selection. To be sure, we need to be initiated into scientific practice to recognize evidence for electrons or the chemical character of water. But the world grounds and constrains what that initiation allows us to say in a way it does not for values.[35]

But if we make up values, how can they be objective? Aren't we just deciding that this or that value exists without anything constraining our decision? And wouldn't this make values arbitrary? If the universe is silent about values, if they come solely from us, then in what sense are they anything other than subjective, or subjective to a particular group (what is sometimes called intersubjective or culturally relative)?

The position I would like to stake out is, at first glance, not a very promising one. I will argue both that we make up values and that they are not arbitrary. Our values are constrained, but not by the material world. They are constrained by the very practices through which we make them up. As might already be guessed, this will involve a rethinking of what it means to say that we make up a value. It is not as simple as saying that *I* make it up or that any particular group of I's make it up. Values come from us, but not in a simple way. That is where all the difficulties lie.

For some, the idea that values come from us and are not to be found in the world or the universe is simply not enough. In their eyes, Camus's view holds sway: if the universe does not give us meaning then there just isn't any. There cannot be meaning, human or otherwise, in a silent universe. These are people for whom the loss of a telos or of God to ground meaning condemns us to nihilism, to the idea that nothing is ultimately better or worse than anything else. As the brother Ivan lamented in *The Brothers Karamazov*, "If God is dead, everything is permitted." To people who hold this view, I have nothing to provide in the way of counsel. Meaningfulness, like morality, is a human product. This does not make it arbitrary. But it does root it in something less sturdy than some would prefer. If anything less than the imprimatur of the universe cancels the possibility of meaningfulness, then my account falls short. But I think it provides a more fulfilling account of meaning than Camus may have envisioned in his despairing moments.

What the account does provide is much of what is attractive about objectivity. In particular, it allows us to give reasons for what we believe about values and, related to this, it allows us to be correct or mistaken in those beliefs. In particular, we might be correct or mistaken not only in applying a value to someone or in saying what criteria a value has but also in our belief about whether something really is a value. We will focus on narrative values, but the account I offer here can hold for other kinds of values as well, in particular moral or aesthetic values.

In approaching this account, let us start simply. Where, one might ask, do values come from? We certainly don't make them up as we go along. It is not as though I decide that, for instance, courage is a value, and then tell everyone else about it. To see why not, imagine deciding that something is a value where nobody else had a reason to think it was one. Imagine, for instance, that I were to declare that walking sideways was a value. People who walk sideways, I announce, are exhibiting a virtue that makes them better people. To stick with meaningfulness, let's imagine that I were to declare that walking sideways lent meaning to a life. How would others around me likely react?

They might start by saying that I was mistaken. Walking sideways just isn't a value that lends meaning to a life. But they would likely say more than this. The idea is not just wrong;

it is ridiculous. For someone to declare walking sideways to be a value indicates that my thinking has gone far astray. I just don't understand, they might say, the kind of things that might give value to a life. There are certain things that might be candidates for giving life meaning, and other things that just don't. When I say, for instance, that subtlety is a narrative value that contributes to the meaningfulness of a life, it is possible that you disagree. You might think that intensity or steadfastness are narrative values, but disagree that subtlety is. But you wouldn't think that it is just crazy to propose subtlety in the way it would be crazy to propose walking sideways as a candidate for meaningfulness.

Take another example. Suppose that I were to propose that henceforth soccer should be played without goalies. The reason for this is that without goalies soccer would be a more high-scoring and therefore more exciting game. You might disagree with me on this, but you would be able to see my point. But suppose instead that I were to suggest that soccer be played on giant fields without any boundaries, that there be no out-of-bounds in soccer except where the giant field ends. And suppose you asked me why I think this would be a good idea, and I replied, "Well, it would give the players more room to run around." That idea seems foolish, and the reason I gave for it won't help convince you otherwise.

Why not? What makes the proposal about the giant field so much more bizarre than the proposal about eliminating the role of goalies?

The proposal to eliminate goalies displays some familiarity with soccer as a particular form of competition. It shows a sense of the game. It is a game that often has lulls, where the strategy is either entirely defensive or at least not overtly aggressive. Forbidding anyone to use her hands to protect the goal would change that dynamic of the game. It might result in less consideration being given to how to stop the other team from scoring and more consideration being given as to how to score more. To think this way is to display a knowledge of how the game unfolds. You might not agree, either that the change would be a good idea or that it might result in more scoring. But these are points we could discuss within a common understanding of how soccer works.

By contrast, extending the field indefinitely doesn't contribute to anything that soccer is about. In fact, it is more likely to destroy the game, since, to avoid being scored on, people could kick the ball hundreds of yards away from the goals. And the idea that the *reason* to extend the field is that it allows players more room doesn't correspond to any aspect of soccer as a game. If someone were to propose that, I would be tempted to ask, "Do you know what soccer is?"

(I should note that one doesn't need to be an expert in soccer to be able to make such judgments. For my own part, I coached my youngest son's recreational soccer team for several years. In my last season of coaching I was approached by one of the other fathers who offered to show me a few formations. My response to this was, "What's a formation?" Now you know why that was my last season of coaching.)

In both cases, soccer and meaningfulness, we have a sense of the difference between a reasonable but perhaps mistaken suggestion and one that is just batty. The former displays a recognition of the kind of thing that might count as a suggestion, given what is at stake. It is offered on the basis of one's possessing a sense of how things in that arena operate. The latter displays no sense of that. A batty suggestion seems to come from nowhere and to intersect with nothing relevant to the issue, whether it be a game or what might lend a life meaning.

But in order to be able to make this distinction, we must already have on hand a sense of what is at stake. We have to be familiar with how things go in soccer or in meaningfulness. In the case of soccer, we know broadly how the game is structured, what the point of it is, how its different rules hang together, and so forth. We might say that we have a sense of the practice as a whole. On the basis of this, we can develop a feel for how a suggested change might impact the game. And, in turn, on the basis of how it might impact the game we can ask (and perhaps even disagree) about whether that impact would contribute to the game or detract from it. Someone who didn't know anything about soccer wouldn't be able to do this. That person would also not be in a position to distinguish why getting rid of goalies might be a mistake, while widening the field indefinitely would be loopy.

Before turning to values and then to meaningfulness, let's stay with the soccer example another moment in order to see a deeper point. Soccer, like all games, is made up. Its rules are made up, and when those rules are modified, the modifications are made up. But soccer is also an evolving game. It is not simply a matter of the particular rules as they stand at a given moment. If the game of soccer consisted only of the set of rules in place at a particular time, then as soon as there was any modification of those rules, there would be a new and different game. But that can't be right.

For instance, in the mid-nineteenth century (but not formalized until 1948), the offside rule was adopted. That is the rule that, roughly, a player on offense cannot stand between the last defensive player and the goal when another offensive player behind him starts to pass to him. The rule assists the defense in the face of an offensive challenge. It is a real change to the game, eliminating a lot of potential offensive strategy. But nobody would argue that the introduction of the offside rule changed soccer into a different game.

Why not? Because soccer is not reducible to a particular set of rules. It is a general practice that involves rules, strategies, and a sense of how the game ought to go. It may be that one of the rules fails to contribute to the game's going as people sense it should, and so the rule is eliminated. Or it may be, as with the offside rule, that a new rule is introduced that might improve the game. It may even be that as the game evolves and circumstances change, things happen that require rule modifications. In basketball, when Wilt Chamberlain started to play professionally several rules had to be changed in order to stop him from utterly dominating the sport. Games like soccer and basketball are not simply sets of rules, then, but practices that respond and evolve within a general sense of the point of the whole practice.

Moreover, the way these responses and evolutions occur cannot be deduced from the rules of the practice at a given moment. They are not like logical or mathematical proofs where the rule changes just follow from the previous rules. It is not as though the offside rule was somehow missing from the other rules and just needed to be added. And it is not as though it was the only rule that could be added that would assist the defense; other rules might have worked just as well. Rather, given the circumstances and a sense of the game, the offside rule seemed to do the trick.

What holds for soccer and basketball also holds for the

other practices in our lives, from teaching to building construction to child rearing to psychotherapy to car driving to relationship building to managerial consulting and so on. Our practices are what we might call open wholes, with various rules and norms and strategies for successful participation, all of which happen with a sense of how the practice in general is supposed to go. Many of the elements of the practice can be questioned or put under scrutiny without the practice being threatened. But not all of them, of course. If we extend the field of play for soccer indefinitely, we no longer have soccer. In order to keep the practice, the elements questioned or changed have to respond to the practice as a whole. One can introduce the notion of the unconscious into psychotherapy without its becoming something other than psychotherapy, but one can't eliminate the role of the therapist and still have the same practice. One can suggest that children need more positive reinforcement if they are to grow up to be healthy, but to suggest that children be asked to count backward from one hundred all day, or walk around in tiny circles, as an aid to their development provides evidence that one just does not understand the practice of child rearing.

Proposing changes to practices, then, happens against a background that has two crucial elements. First, those changes do not necessarily derive from the rules or norms of the practice as they are currently constructed. Proposed changes do not have to be simply extensions or clarifications of the rules of a practice as it stands. Second, those changes, if they are to make sense, must be responsive to a sense of the practice as a whole. The difference between proposing a change to a practice and proposing something that will either destroy or lie entirely outside the practice consists in whether the proposed change can make sense within the context in which the practice is being, well, practiced. To put this last point another way, one can give reasons for the proposed change that will be recognized by those in the practice (or at least many of them) as responding to aspects of the practice.

The rule changes we have been considering seek to make practices better, and in various ways. The offside rule sought to make soccer *fairer* for the defense. A rule that prohibited goalies would hope to make soccer *more exciting*. The rule changes in basketball when Wilt Chamberlain entered the league made play *fairer* for the other players. Introducing the idea of the unconscious was supposed to (although in the end did not) make psychotherapy *more accurate* in its approach. Other proposed changes to other practices could contribute in other ways. The change in voting practices introduced by women's suffrage made that practice *more democratic*. Integrating rest or play periods into work is sometimes said to make it *more efficient*.

And it is not just rule changes that can have these effects on practices. Technological developments can have widespread effects: the invention of the printing press made literacy *more democratic*, as did the development of the Internet for various practices of knowledge. Innovations within a practice, such as the introduction of light into painting by the impressionists or rap by hip-hop artists, can make that practice *more interesting*. Importing elements from other practices into a practice can have positive consequences as well. Integrating film clips into teaching practices (which itself was made possible by technological innovations) sometimes makes learning *more relevant* to students. Bringing dance steps into exercise routines, the way Jazzercise does, can make workouts *more fun*.

What do fairness, accuracy, excitement, democracy, efficiency, interest, relevance, and fun have in common in these different developments? They are all values. They are all measures of various kinds by which a practice might be assessed as being better or worse. A political practice like suffrage can be made better by being made more democratic, art is generally improved when it allows for developments that make it more interesting, and sports are improved when they are made fairer. To be sure, not all values attach to all practices. It would rarely be considered an improvement of any relevant kind to make politics more fun (although perhaps at the moment a little levity might not hurt, given the rabid polarization of politics in the United States). Instead, what values count as relevant depend on the character of the practices themselves. And that character is not a matter simply of the rules, but of the practice as a whole.

But if the changes proposed to these various practices are supposed to promote particular values, it is possible that they will not. Whether or not they will is a matter that can be argued about. We can give reasons for or against them, either before their introduction or after we see their effects. There are those who argue that the introduction of rap into contemporary music made it not more interesting but in fact more boring and repetitive. And there are those who might claim that eliminating the role of the goalie in soccer would not make it more exciting but instead just result in too many goals scored without enough thoughtful strategy, which is actually less exciting.

These arguments need not be arbitrary matters of opinion. One could bring reasons to bear on either side of the debate, and it might be possible to settle a debate on the basis of those reasons. Looking at the evolving character of rap music, one could make a strong case that, gangster rap and mindless corporate appropriations of rap notwithstanding, it has over the past several decades added a dimension and opened up possibilities for music that were not there before. And if the goalie were eliminated from soccer for a while, it might be possible to get a sense of whether the game became more or less exciting and more or less compelling for those who follow it.

But there is more. Beyond a reasoned discussion about whether proposed changes will contribute to certain values, one can even debate the values themselves. It can be asked whether this or that value is a good one for the practice to express, or whether or not there needs to be more of it. For instance, it could be argued that psychotherapy does not need to be more accurate. (My wife does psychotherapy, so I hear about these discussions secondhand.) The point of psychotherapy, some say, is not to get a correct picture of how someone's mind is working but instead to help him adjust in ways that make his life go better. It is to offer a way to frame a person's experience so that he can go on without feeling stuck or unhappy or anxious. The goal isn't that the frame be inaccurate rather than accurate; it is that accuracy does not matter either way. The point of therapy, these people argue, is cure rather than insight. Cure is defined in terms of better living in the eyes of the client. If insight does not lead to a cure then it is useless.

Others, of course, disagree. They argue that a proper cure requires accurate insight, or that insight is valuable on its own. I am not in a position to solve this debate. What makes it relevant for us is that it is not a debate about whether certain changes in the practice of psychotherapy will realize a particular value—accuracy—but whether the value itself worth realizing. This discussion is not arbitrary, because it refers to the goals of the practice itself. I suppose that everyone who does psychotherapy thinks that better living is at least part of the point of the practice. But there can be debates not only about whether accurate insight leads to better living but about whether it has any value at all aside from being a means, and perhaps a dubious one, for psychotherapy to promote personal thriving. There can be disagreement about whether the ancient dictum to "know thyself" should be a value embraced in the practice of therapy.

Even if someone embraces the value expressed in a practice, she could argue that there need be neither more nor less of it introduced at a particular time: that everything is fine as it stands. We can easily imagine a soccer fan saying this about a proposal to eliminate the role of goalie. Suppose a soccer fan said something like this: "Yes, I agree that getting rid of goalies would make soccer more exciting. But soccer is exciting enough the way it is. Right now, instead of all kinds of action we have a slow tension throughout much of the match. It explodes every once in a while when there is a goal or a near goal. That is the perfect rhythm for a soccer match to have. Ratcheting up the excitement level would destroy this rhythm that we like."

This is a different complaint about the proposal to eliminate goalies from the one that denies that it will make the game more exciting. In the first case, the criticism is that it won't in fact accomplish the goal of increasing excitement. All those goals will get boring after a while. The special excitement that comes with scoring a goal will be lost. This new complaint concedes that there might be more excitement without a goalie, but that there doesn't need to be any more.

Adding more excitement would detract from other elements of the game, specifically its rhythm of tension and release.

As with the psychotherapy case, the debate about whether soccer should become more exciting can be a reasonable one. It does not have to be arbitrary. This debate would likely touch upon deep questions about the nature and point of the game. What is it that fans respond to about soccer? What makes it compelling for them? How do they see soccer matches in relation to their emotional lives? Is it supposed to be relaxing, hectic, dramatic, or something else? It might be difficult to get agreement on these issues, but a discussion about them need not be simply a matter of personal opinion. And after all, many discussions about more important issues (if that phrase is not too offensive to soccer fans) are difficult to find agreement on, but not for that reason considered matters solely of personal opinion.

There is more still. Not only can a proposal for a change be offered or challenged in the name of a value, and not only can values be challenged from the standpoint of other values in a practice, but an entire practice can be challenged from the perspective of another practice. One can bring reasons to bear from the standpoint of a particular practice to criticize a different one. This might seem like a far-fetched possibility, but it is actually not so difficult to imagine.

Much of my background in philosophy is in French philosophy. One of the figures I have spent the most time studying is the recent thinker Michel Foucault. He is often dismissed by academics because his thought is fashionable and, frankly, because he was French. In academic philosophy in particular, being French counts as a strike against one, and being both fashionable and French counts as two strikes. Foucault's thought, however, seems at least initially to be standing the test of time. He was not only a philosopher but also a historian, and he used history to raise questions about both philosophical and nonphilosophical practices. His histories attempt to show that what are often taken to be natural or universal elements of human experience turn out to be historical products. In other words, things weren't always the way they are now. Which means that things don't always have to be this way. We can change what seems to be natural or inescapable.

Foucault's most influential work is *Discipline and Punish*. It recounts the rise of the prison, particularly but not exclusively in France. In this rise, the practice of rehabilitation rather than mere brute punishment begins to take hold. This would seem like a good idea. After all, isn't rehabilitation a way of giving people a future that mere punishment would not? Foucault is not so sanguine about this. For him, rehabilitation, especially through the practice of psychology and psychotherapy, is not so much liberating as normalizing. By normalizing he means molding people's behavior and conception of themselves along narrow predefined pathways. Rehabilitation does not so much offer a future for one to remake oneself in a healthier way; rather, it constrains people to act in accordance with the needs of an industrial capitalist society. Foucault shows this by tracing the rise of various practices in the prison that mold behavior: training the body for repetitive tasks, minute observation of prisoners' lives, and constant judgment against standards of the normal. Moreover, these practices do not remain locked inside the prison gates. They migrate out and help contribute to a sanitized and normalized society.

Psychology, in his view, lies at the root of this normalizing endeavor. It seeks to create the know-how to constrain people's lives. "Is this the birth of the sciences of man?" he asks, answering, "It is probably to be found in these 'ignoble' archives, where the modern play of coercion over bodies, gestures, and behavior has its beginnings."[36] For Foucault, the practices of psychology, psychiatry, and psychotherapy (along with related disciplines like sociology) are inseparable from the prison's efforts to fit people who have committed crimes back into society in a way that maintains order, rather than offering them a chance to create themselves.

As with the previous examples, whether Foucault is right in his historical critique of rehabilitation and psychology is subject to reasonable debate. That debate would marshal various historical facts about the prisons and psychology as well as more speculative questions about the effects of these practices. However, whether Foucault is ultimately vindicated, the example of his work shows that one can criticize an entire practice or complex of practices—in this case rehabilitation and psychology—from the standpoint of another practice— in this case history aligned with a progressive political view. From Foucault's perspective, if it is valuable that people get to determine the shape of their own lives, then rehabilitation and psychological practice are inimical to that value. His history of their emergence and their effects seeks to show this. His work, then, is an example of how entire practices can be subject to criticism and challenge—but only from the perspective of other practices that are endorsed by the critic.

Let's take stock for a moment. We have seen that aspects of particular practices can be criticized or defended on the basis of certain values. We have also seen that those values themselves can be criticized or defended on the basis of other values in a practice. And we have seen that entire practices, along with their values, can be criticized or defended on the basis of the values associated with other practices. All of this criticizing and defending can be done rationally; that is, one can give reasons for what one says. It does not have to be solely a matter of personal opinion, like which flavor of ice cream one prefers. What is characteristic of these reasons is that they invoke particular values: the values on the basis of which to modify practices, the values on the basis of which to criticize other values in a practice, and the values on the basis of which to criticize the values of a different practice. To put the point another way, in order for reasoned debate to occur about what is better and what is worse, some values have to be held constant. They can't be put into question, since they are the reasons one gives for criticizing other values or other practices.

This is what is sometimes called holism. The philosopher Wilfrid Sellars once wrote, in a quote that has become famous in recent philosophy, that "empirical knowledge, like its sophisticated extension, science, is rational, not because it has a *foundation* but because it is a self-correcting enterprise which can put *any* claim in jeopardy, though not *all* at once."[37] I am arguing that the same thing happens—or at least *can* happen—with regard to values. There is no foundation of values that everyone must agree on, but that does not mean that our values are arbitrary. They can be scrutinized, criticized, modified, and defended. In order to do so, however, other values have to be taken as a standard. One can't hold all values up for examination at the same time.

What would a foundation for our knowledge or our values look like? It would be what we were seeking in the first chapter. It would be a guarantee that knowledge or values are founded in something firm and unyielding, like God or Aristotle's cosmos. It would be what Camus thought was necessary to escape the meaninglessness of life. But we can't have that. For Sellars, the reason we can't have that is that there is no foundation for empirical knowledge of the kind philosophers like Descartes sought. And we can't have it for values of meaningfulness either, for reasons we have already seen. Sellars's insight was that the either/or option—either knowledge has a foundation or we can't justify what we think we know—is false. There is a third option. This option is holistic: we can question any part of the whole network of knowledge, but not the whole itself. Something has to be held constant in order for the questioning to make sense.

The view I am presenting here, which owes a deep debt to the work of Sellars and his students,[38] holds that what goes for knowledge also goes for values. Values are not arbitrary. They are responsive to reasons. They can be invoked to scrutinize practices, and they can in turn be subject to scrutiny themselves. They are part of a network that is anchored by the complex web of practices that constitute our lives. There is nothing beneath that web that would serve as a foundation for it, ultimately justifying it from the standpoint of the universe. But that does not mean that all claims of value are arbitrary. Even if we can't stand outside the web itself and offer it up for an audit, we can, from within it, assess our values and our practices.

If this is right, then we can say both that our values are made up and that they are, in an important way, objective. They aren't arbitrary, and they respond to reasons. But, as I indicated at the outset of this chapter, to say this involves rethinking what it means to make up a value. The image we have when we say that someone is making up a value is that it is something an individual can do by herself: it is purely up to the person making it up whether it is really a value or not. The picture I have painted here denies this. Whether something is a value can be subject to discussion based on the values and practices of the group or community in which it arises. This does not mean that if it conflicts with another value already held by those in that community it is necessarily mistaken. It can be that, upon reflection, the value that was previously held cannot withstand scrutiny. (As Sellars says, any claim can be in jeopardy, but not all of them at once.) But in order for a proposed value actually to be one, it must find its place in the web of values and practices that constitute a community's life.

There is also a deeper point here. Not only can an individual not make up a value in the sense of simply declaring it to be one; neither can an entire community do this. Values cannot be made up by a group any more than they can be made up by an individual. Values are neither subjective nor, in the term I used earlier, intersubjective. Not only are individuals enmeshed in the web of values and practices in which they are involved; the entire community constituted by those values and practices is just as bound to them. A group or community cannot simply make up or declare something to be a value without its being anchored in at least some of the values it already holds. To try to do that would be like a group, instead of an individual, declaring that walking sideways was a value. Such a declaration wouldn't make sense even to the group declaring it. It might be fun to play as a game. But it couldn't be taken seriously as a value.

In order to arrive at an adequate grasp of how narrative values fit into this picture, we have to add one more element. There are some values that apply not only *within* practices but also *across* them. These are values that seem to be relevant no matter what practice one is engaged in. One example of these is moral values. Values like honesty, courage, and respect for others seem to apply to participation in all practices. Whether it is soccer, child rearing, teaching, or accounts receivable, moral values are thought relevant to the way one goes about engaging in one's practices.

This does not mean that moral values must always dominate the other values of the practice. As is said in philosophy, moral values do not necessarily trump other values. In business and in soccer, for instance, it can be permissible to be dishonest in certain ways, leading a competitor to think one is doing one thing when, in actuality, one is preparing for something else. In soccer a team can feint moving into a defensive formation, and then all of a sudden attack the opponent's goal. In business it is okay to make a competitor think one is going to move into a certain market, and then move into a different one.

But even in cases like these, honesty is still relevant in a more general way. There might be particular ways in which dishonesty is allowed in soccer and in business, but everyone recognizes that dishonesty has certain boundaries. Pretending that one has been fouled in soccer, although not uncommon, is considered cheating. Spreading false rumors about the dangerousness of a competitor's product is morally out of bounds in business. The value of honesty, then, although it can be limited in particular ways in our practices, is always relevant to them.

Narrative values function in much the same way. They are relevant to us across our practices, but in a different way from moral values. Moral values are relevant to each practice we engage in. Narrative values are relevant both to the kinds of practices each of us chooses to engage in and the ways we engage in them. This is just another way of saying that narrative values are relevant to our lives as we live them over time. Rather than asking whether our engagement in a particular practice is honest or courageous or patient or respectful, we ask whether our lives are adventurous or steadfast or expressive of personal integrity or intellectual curiosity. Just as moral values are relevant across the practices that people participate in, narrative values are relevant across the practices that *I* engage in over the course of my life.

The idea that there are certain values, like moral values and narrative ones, that are relevant across practices might appear to make them immune to criticism or scrutiny. It seems to remove them from the web or the whole that we have been discussing. This appearance would be misleading. To say that moral or narrative values are, in their different ways, relevant across practices is not to say that they somehow lie beneath or outside or above our practices. They have to answer to the practices with which they are engaged just as other values do. And they can be criticized or limited from the perspective of those practices. Just as one can criticize the proposal to eliminate the role of the goalie from soccer as destroying the rhythm of the game, so one could criticize a proposal to make soccer more honest by disallowing strategies that rely on leading a team to think one is moving into a defensive formation while preparing an attack.

Imagine what it would be like if we made soccer as honest as we could. There would be no fake passes, no fancy footwork with the ball, and no deceptive formations. If we were going to be really honest, we might have to tell the opponent when we were thinking of trying to score and when we were content to play defense. And they, of course, would have to tell all that to us. What would be left of soccer then?

The fact that values like moral or narrative ones can apply across practices, then, does not mean that they are immune from criticism. They can be criticized from the perspective of the practice in which they are being applied. Moreover, there is an entire practice from which moral and narrative values can be reflected upon and scrutinized. That practice is philosophy. In doing philosophy we can ask about the value of honesty or courage or subtlety or adventurousness in general, not just in their relation to specific practices. Asking about the importance of honesty in a philosophical way is in one way like asking about the importance of excitement in the game of soccer. In both cases, the investigation is holistic in the way we described above. We hold certain things constant in order to ask about honesty or excitement. In soccer, we hold constant the other elements of the game. In philosophy, we hold constant other moral values in the general philosophical framework. In each case, a particular value is being held up for investigation on the basis of the other commitments of the practice. The difference is that in soccer we are asking about the importance of excitement for the game, while in philosophy we are asking about the importance of honesty in general, and not just for philosophy.

The objectivity of our values, then, lies in the whole, not in any particular belief. It is within the entire web of beliefs that reasons take place and that people can be justified or not. It is the web that grounds our scrutiny of our lives, our practices, and indeed our values. No value, narrative or otherwise, must be accepted solely on the basis that a person or a community believes it. It is compelling—if indeed it is—because it makes sense within the network of values in which it seeks to find a place, a network each of whose other values has no more sturdy grounding than it does.

This has important implications for narrative values. There can be several ways a group or community could be wrong about a narrative value it holds. First, it could be mistaken in believing that a particular person is actually exhibiting a narrative value. Everybody could think that someone is exhibiting a narrative value even when she is not. Second, it could be mistaken about the proper criteria for a narrative value. Everyone in a group could agree on the criteria for a narrative value, and then later come to realize that they were confused or incorrect. Third, a group or community could be mistaken about whether something is a narrative value in the first place. It could hold something to be a narrative value which it later comes to think was not. Alternatively, a previously unrecognized narrative value can come to be acknowledged as one. Let's look at an example of each in order to see how the objectivity of narrative values operates.

Suppose that a community agrees that a particular person is steadfast in her commitments. She displays the behavior of steadfastness across various aspects of her life, and has done so for a long time. Those who interact with her are not hesitant to call her steadfast. She sticks by her commitments without fail, no matter how difficult they seem. There are even times when it seems reasonable for her to let a commitment lapse without consequence; yet nevertheless she sees it through. She risks travel through a dangerous snow to appear at dinner with a friend when she could have easily rearranged it. She works through the night to finish a report for which she would have been granted extra time had she only asked. Periodically she canvasses her commitments in her head to ensure that she doesn't forget any of them, no matter how trivial.

Let's also suppose, however, that our purportedly steadfast person is driven by compulsions that nobody, including her, is aware of. Perhaps this is because the community in which she lives is ignorant of such compulsions. It does not have the psychological resources to notice it. Nobody has ever been diagnosed with anything like obsessive-compulsive disorder, and its symptoms have always been taken to be marks of a particularly stringent kind of steadfastness. And while this person herself maybe feels a bit overly constrained by her behavior, even at times tortured by it, the praise she receives for her steadfastness gives her to understand herself in a largely positive light, and so she has no reason to think of herself as having a problem.

Later, however, the development of psychological knowledge in the community leads to the recognition that what looks like dogged steadfastness is sometimes a display of something more compulsive. The community then agrees that what seemed to be her steadfastness turned out to be something else. This does not mean that this person comes to be seen as sick rather than admirable. The attitude toward her could be more nuanced than that. There is no reason to believe that she does not care for her friends or her work. But that care is embedded in a condition that owes more to psychological difficulty than to a narrative value.

This is an example of how a group or community could be mistaken in applying the criteria for a particular narrative value. The community understood the criteria that constitutes steadfastness, but erroneously thought that what they were seeing was an instance of it. Had the members of this community had knowledge of obsessive-compulsive disorders, it might have approached its judgment of her behavior differently.

But now it might be asked whether the criteria themselves could be mistaken. Could a group be wrong not just in its judgment of whether someone is exhibiting a narrative value but about the benchmarks it uses for a narrative value? That is to say, could a community be correct in thinking that something was a narrative value but wrong in some aspect of what that value consists in, some element of its nature or makeup?

Again the answer is yes. As an example, we can turn to the value of subtlety. Imagine that a society valued subtlety, but thought that if people of a certain class, say the aristocratic class, did not understand the signals one sent out through one's behavior, then they weren't really subtle. Indirect communication that could be understood only by the elite was considered a necessary element of being subtle. This, however, changed over time. With the rise of a more democratic aura, subtlety became a matter of understated behavior whose significance might be understood by anyone who was attentive. And later, looking back at its history, people in the community said something to themselves like, "We thought that subtlety was only a matter of signals traveling among the elite, but now we know better."

Or imagine this: during the time when subtlety was thought to lie in the province of the aristocratic class, someone challenged the more restrictive criterion on the basis that it failed to understand the character of subtlety. He argued that there are all kinds of ways to exhibit subtle signals, and that those ways were not significantly different from what passed for subtlety among the elite. For instance, while a slight upward tilt of the head indicated agreement among the elite, a slight nod among those in other classes indicated the same type of agreement. Or while a certain way of playing one's hand at bridge would signal one's strategy to a partner perceptive enough to recognize it, there were also signals given in working-class card games that came through in the way hands were played.

It could not be said that, simply by opposing the criteria that were currently in place, this critic would be mistaken. Perhaps people would come to think that they had been inaccurate in believing that subtlety was restricted to certain class understandings. Or perhaps people would fail to realize that they were inaccurate, but nevertheless they were, since the critic was right in thinking that they were confused in their understanding of what subtlety consisted in. They would be wrong by their own lights, even if they didn't realize it, since the critic was appealing in a holistic way to their general understanding of subtlety. But they failed to understand this, since the traditional view had too strong a grip on them.

Finally, not only the application or the criteria for narrative values could be mistaken. Narrative values themselves could emerge that hadn't previously been recognized, or they could drop out, or they could be challenged in a reasonable manner. One might argue, for instance, that subtlety itself is too elitist or too cliquish a value to lend objective meaningfulness to a life. If one sought to refute this challenge, it would not be enough to say, "You're wrong *because* the rest of us have agreed that it is a narrative value." There would have to be reasons offered, and it is unclear at the outset where the exchange of reasons would lead. Any reasons that were offered would have to appeal to a network or web of reasons already in place to which one could appeal; debates such as this would have to take place in a context that itself remained more or less constant during the discussion. But the values themselves cannot be defended merely on the basis that they are currently accepted. "You're wrong because we believe you're wrong" is not a refutation.

Finally, it is possible to argue for the existence of a narrative value that had not previously been recognized. This, of course, is the opposite of arguing against a value a community holds. But it is equally conceivable. I suspect, for instance, that intensity as a narrative value is of more recent vintage. It has probably emerged as a value in modern life as access to different activities has increased. Where once the idea of intensity might have had no grip on a society in which loyalty or steadfastness were more dominant values, in a world in which people can choose to throw themselves into something it emerges as a source of meaningfulness.

This should not be taken to mean that people who lived intensely during a time in which intensity was not recognized as a value did not in fact express that value in their lives. Recall that people can express a narrative value without recognizing it. Someone's expressing intensity in her life before anyone recognized it as a value would be in the same position. And although at the time nobody would have said that someone expressing intensity was living a meaningful life (assuming they had the concepts of meaningfulness and perhaps a few other narrative values, such as steadfastness), they would have been mistaken. Her intense life, as long as she was subjectively engaged with it, would have been a meaningful one. The fact that nobody, including her, would have known this would have no more bearing than the fact that nobody knew that the earth was round would have made the earth any flatter.

By whose lights would we make this judgment of meaningfulness? By our lights, of course. What other lights would there be by which we could make it? We judge that this person's life was meaningful in much the same way as we judge the earth to be spherical: by means of the web of reasons that is our inheritance. This does not mean that these reasons are infallible. It could be that, through another turn in history, we (or those who follow us) come to think that intensity really isn't a value. Perhaps reasons will emerge that we hadn't considered before that convince us of this. Then we will come to think that we were mistaken and that this poor woman's life was, sadly, without much meaning. But the fact that it is conceivable that we might one day come to think this gives us no reason to think it now. All of our reasons, or at least the weight of them—assuming you agree with me that intensity is a narrative value—point toward the meaningfulness of a life at a time when it might not have been recognized as such. And what do we have to rely on except the weight of our current reasons?

There is a worry here that might have crept in for some readers as this discussion has unfolded. It is a worry that is particularly relevant to moral values, but might be applied to narrative values as well. If moral (or narrative) values are tied to practices, does that mean that there are no universal values? Is morality or meaningfulness relative to the practices of a particular group or community or culture? Is there no such thing as human morality or human meaningfulness in general?

This is a particularly disturbing concern when it comes to morality. If there is no universal morality, it would seem that we would be unable to criticize cultures that engage in what seem like egregious practices. It is the problem of relativism.

For instance, there are still a few cultures in which women are subjected to clitoridectomy, the cutting off of their clitorises. I hope I am not alone in thinking that this is an offensive practice, even more so since many women in these cultures are given no say in the matter. However, if morality is relative to the practices of a particular community—that is, if moral rightness and wrongness are defined within the framework of those practices—then who am I to say that people operating within a context where clitoridectomy is accepted are morally mistaken? Or, to push the problem a bit further, how would I criticize the Nazi who said that in Nazi culture the killing of people considered to be inferior was held to be an important moral task?

Fortunately for us, we do not have to solve this vexed problem, since morality is not our concern.[39] With regard to meaningfulness, the situation is complicated enough. In order to ask about the narrative values of another culture, we would first have to ask whether they have any concepts like those of meaningfulness and any values that seemed to correspond to our narrative values. Suppose they did. Then we could ask, from our cultural context, whether those values are anything like ours, and whether, if they were not, we had good reason to say they are correct or mistaken. All of this, like the historical case we just considered, must take place from our own standpoint. From where else could it take place? We can't judge other values without having some values to hold constant: this is the lesson of holism. So if we could find analogies to narrative values, we could ask about them, give reasons for or against them, and come to some judgment about them. It might be that we find their values to be mistaken. But it also might be that their thinking about narrative values has something to teach us, and that we were mistaken in our own thinking about them. We cannot say in advance where such a conversation would lead. This, too, is a lesson of holism.

But suppose that this other culture didn't possess anything similar or analogous to our conceptions of meaningfulness and narrative values. Would that imply that their lives were meaningless? It would not. It would be almost the same case as that of the woman who lived intensely in a culture that had not yet recognized it as a narrative value. The only difference would be that in this case there weren't *any* values that were recognized as conferring meaningfulness on someone's life. However, as we have seen, a person can live a perfectly meaningful life without ever asking whether it is meaningful. What is required is subjective engagement in a way that expresses a narrative value. But the person does not need to know that she is expressing a narrative value in order to do so. Moreover, recall the case of my uncle, who persistently thought he was being subtle when in fact his life was an expression of a very unsubtle caring for those around him. We can say of those in other cultures what we might say of people in our own: that they are living meaningful lives even though they don't recognize it.

And we should bear in mind that the proposal that narrative values offer objective criteria for thinking about meaningfulness does not preclude that there might be other ways of thinking about meaningfulness. I am not aware of any, but that hardly counts against the possibility. What I have defended in this book is a particular way of thinking about meaning, one that I hope will help people take stock of their lives in a fruitful way. But it might be that in conversation with other cultures or even other communities, we (whoever this "we" happens to be) come to understand that there are other ways of living meaningfully besides that of expressing narrative values. On the holistic view this is not impossible.

In fact, my very project counts on it. What I have tried to do here is to convince you that, given a general web of beliefs that we share, there is a set of values that lend meaningfulness to a life that you might not have previously recognized or considered. I have done this by appealing to beliefs that I hope you already share, beliefs about the criteria for what might count as meaningfulness, about the significance of thinking of meaning in terms of a life trajectory, and about the importance of values like intensity, steadfastness, intellectual curiosity, and the lot. Without this common web of beliefs, my project here would never get off the ground. (In fact, without a common web of beliefs, it is unclear how we could talk convincingly with one another about anything at all.)

But here someone might ask, what justifies the web itself? If we accept or reject certain values based on the web of beliefs a community holds, how do we know the web itself is right? It may be that values aren't arbitrary because they must be justified within the network of other values and practices. But couldn't the entire thing be arbitrary? And if it is, doesn't that, by extension, make each of the values in it arbitrary?

The worry here is that our web of values, founded in our practices, is somehow floating in space. It is unmoored. Without being anchored somewhere, it could be floating anywhere: that is the arbitrariness of it. If the web is what anchors the values, but the web is unanchored, then each of the values still floats free—not from the web, but along with it.

The short response to this worry is this: nothing justifies the web.

We have arrived at the point where justification comes to an end. In fact, we have arrived at the point where justification *must* come to an end. We cannot justify the web, the whole, itself. The reason for this is that all justification, all giving of reasons for what one believes, happens inside the web. This is true not only for values but for all of our beliefs. Recall that the citation from Wilfrid Sellars referred not to values but instead to empirical beliefs, and said the same of science: "Empirical knowledge, like its sophisticated extension, science, is rational, not because it has a *foundation* but because it is a self-correcting enterprise which can put *any* claim in jeopardy, though not *all* at once." The attempt to step outside our current web of beliefs, values, and the practices in which they arise in order to justify the whole is an impossible task. After all, what would even count as a justification for an empirical claim or a value if we need to lay aside everything else we believe? In a case like that, it would be the claim or value itself that would be floating free, unanchored to anything else.

Now one might object here that, at least with science, there is something that anchors its claims: the world itself. While our values might be unmoored, don't our scientific beliefs have to answer to the way the world is arranged, independent of us? To answer this question adequately would take us deep into issues in the philosophy of science. Let me just offer the following as a suggestion: although our scientific beliefs do have to answer to the world, the ways they do so are still within the network of our beliefs. No single scientific claim confronts the world in some bald fashion: a lone belief over here and the world over there. A scientific claim is not just tested in the world; the concepts it uses are a product of the web of beliefs (and even values) that form the context of a scientific practice. As philosophers of science like to say, our observations of the world are themselves "theory laden." That is: they happen against a background web of the practices and commitments of science itself.

If we had a God or a foundation to turn to in order to justify the web itself, that would do the trick. It would offer us a solid ground in which to anchor our practices. It would grant us the cosmic guarantee that would ally all fears of arbitrariness. But we have seen that we cannot justify our values through an appeal to God and that the history of philosophy has not been kind to the idea of foundations. When we seek to justify not this or that value but the entire mesh itself we find ourselves in a position captured in an image from the philosopher Ludwig Wittgenstein: "If I have exhausted the justifications, I have reached bedrock and my spade is turned. Then I am inclined to say: 'This is simply what I do.'"

The image is a striking one, and it is famous in contemporary philosophy. My only quibble with it is that the reference to bedrock suggests that there is hard ground beneath the soil of our practices. But there isn't, as the last line of the citation reminds us. The reason we cannot dig any deeper is that there is no more soil left. This is not because we have hit something sturdy that resists our spade. It is only because we have run out of soil. What is left is not granite or marble; it is nothing. This is simply what we do.

The web of values and beliefs and the practices in which they arise are all we have to ground objectivity. Any one of us could be wrong, and we could all be wrong—although we cannot say why this might be, since that would refer us back to our own practices, beliefs, and justifications. It is perhaps possible that far in the future a generation of posthuman types will look back upon us and ask, "What were they thinking?" Of course, they will do that from their own lights, as we do from ours. And, of course, we cannot imagine what it would be like to be those posthuman types, since we would have to do it from our perspective. All we can say is that we cannot in advance rule out the possibility of it happening.

Our web of practices, with their beliefs and values, does not rest on a ground assured by the universe. As with meaningfulness, the universe is silent on this matter. But neither do the beliefs and values in that web arise simply according to individual or collective whim. When we seek to justify our narrative values (or anything else) to ourselves, we are in a realm which is neither arbitrary nor ultimately assured, but somewhere in between. For some, this might not be enough. And to them, as I have said, I have nothing to offer by way of consolation. But for the rest of us, although this may not be all the objectivity we would like, perhaps it is all the objectivity we need.

CONCLUSION:
NOT EVERYTHING,
BUT SOMETHING

Many of us would have preferred that the universe welcomed us as awaited ones. That it invited us in with an air of expectation fulfilled, and asked of our lives tasks that we would have chosen and that give them meaning. We would have preferred our humanity to be etched into the nature of things as an imprimatur that gives it—and us—significance. Barring that, we would at least have liked a little cosmic support: a God or a telos that assures us of meaningfulness of the years that we spend here.

But things are not like that. The universe is silent. We are not anointed, we are not awaited, and we are not welcomed. As Darwin has taught us, we are evolutionary contingencies. Nothing led to our existence except the changing character of the nonhuman environment. Had an asteroid not crashed into the earth near the Yucatán Peninsula, we might not even be here. We are cosmic accidents.

Worse, even if there is—or were—a God beyond the silence, that would not assure us of meaning. As we have seen, for a life to be meaningful it has to be recognized as meaningful by us. We are implicated in the very concept of meaning. We cannot rely on it, because, to one extent or another, it must rely on us. Meaningfulness, if it exists, is woven into the fabric of our thought about our lives, and cannot be extricated from it.

A silent universe, however, need not leave us destitute. Camus, as we saw at the outset, moved too quickly from the awareness of silence to the despair of meaninglessness. And in philosophical reflection, on our lives or on anything else, the first rule is never to move too quickly. There is always more than meets the eye. The trick is to slow down long enough to see it, to rein in our temptation to assume that the pathways we have already carved for thought are the only ones available to us. Only then can we recognize possibilities that might, beyond our hurry to get on with our lives, reorient how we think about ourselves and our world.

Camus failed to see that there is more to being human than to be a passive recipient of meaning. Perhaps, as he thought, it is nowhere inscribed in the universe. Perhaps it is we who create it. This does not entail that we are utterly bereft. If we investigate our relation to the world, we find riches that might confer a particular kind of splendor to our existence. We find our meaning not beneath or beyond our lives, but within them. There is a meaningfulness—or a potential meaningfulness—that, while not inscribed into the nature of things, emerges from our engagement with those things and their nature.

This meaningfulness does not come in the form of a *what*, but of a *how*. It is not the thing that, dropped into our lives, makes them meaningful. It lies instead in the way we go about being the kinds of creatures we are. It may be individual, allowing us each to navigate the world in our own way without losing access to meaning. But it is also general in the sense that, for there to be meaningfulness, there must be certain themes that are recognizable not only within but across different lives. There are ways of living, ways of taking up the trajectory of our lives, which might merit the name *meaningful*. They lie within the manner in which we inhabit the time allotted to us, the styles we create over the course of our years.

This meaningfulness is more, or other, than happiness. We can be happy without meaning, and our lives can be meaningful without being happy. Although, as we have seen, Daniel Haybron's resonant description of happiness brings it close to the kind of subjective absorption in life that is one side of meaning, there can be still be such engagement without the full-blown happiness he describes; and there can be attunement, engagement, and endorsement without the narrative values that constitute the objective side of meaningfulness.

There can also be meaningfulness without success. We have not touched upon this yet, but in the current context it is worth insisting on the distinction between success and meaningfulness.

Our world, and especially what is sometimes called the "First World," is consumed by prospects of success and fears of failure. Lives seem vindicated by riches or fame or public achievements of one sort or another. These achievements need not amount to much. On TV reality shows, fraught battles for pointless goals are engaged in by individuals whose pride in victory could not contrast more profoundly with the paltriness of their accomplishments. Riches and fame are offered to us as markers of lives worth living, even though we have example after example paraded before us of the misery of many such lives. To be sure, poverty should not be seen as some romantic spur to authenticity. But neither should wealth or popularity be taken as a guarantor of a life worth having lived.

Taped to the top of my computer at work is a quote from the social theorist and art critic John Berger: "We were not somewhere between success and failure; we were elsewhere." University life, no less than other pursuits, is driven by norms of success. Success may be defined differently: it appears less in the form of high salaries (although this is not irrelevant) and more in the form of books and papers published with well-regarded journals or publishers. But it shadows our pursuits nevertheless. I have constantly to remind myself that the reason I threw myself into philosophy was not to achieve acclaim among fellow academics—and still less among academic administrators—but because I wanted to think about who I was and how I should live, and do so in conversation with great minds of the past and present. In the current university environment, my ability to keep this motive front and center is often compromised.

And yet I realize that, in seeking to hew to the lesson of Berger's words, I am luckier than most. I can write about what interests me, and I often have an audience of students with whom to discuss my thoughts. I am not subject to sales or production quotas characteristic of many businesses (although there are forces both inside and outside the university that seek to change that); for my livelihood I do not rely on how many clients I see or how many houses I inspect or how many forms I can push from one side of the desk to the other. If it is difficult for me to contest the norm of success, how much more challenging is it for so many others who have not the good fortune of my position?

However, it is one thing to say that we are too mesmerized by a norm of success. It is another to say how else we might think of ourselves. Narrative values provide an alternative source of such thought. Several of the characters we have canvassed here are examples of narrative expression rather than of success as our culture has sought to define it. Dilsey from Faulkner's *The Sound and the Fury*, the Trappist monks, and my self-deceptive but kind uncle whom we met in chapter 3 are all examples. Claus von Stauffenberg, the German officer who led the failed Operation Valkyrie against Hitler, is another. So are those whose lives are characterized by adventure or intensity or intellectual curiosity or courage but who are never rewarded with wealth or accolades or public recognition.

The philosopher Bernard Williams, in his essay "Moral Luck," imagines a particular Paul Gauguin, one who resembles the great painter Gauguin in many biographical details, but who is given a particular psychological portrait by Williams. His Gauguin would like to do the right thing, to live in a way that would be morally vindicated. Like the real Paul Gauguin, Williams's Gauguin leaves his life as a businessman and his family to paint, eventually moving to Tahiti. The disturbing possibility Williams raises is that this Gauguin is morally justified or not in his decision only after having gone there.[40] He cannot know in advance whether he will be morally justified. It would be only the creation of great art that could vindicate him. This is what makes for the moral luck in the article's title.

I would like to imagine a slightly different Gauguin, one that seeks not to do the right thing but instead to live a meaningful life. Let us suppose that Gauguin takes off to Tahiti, and it turns out he's a bad painter. He's a hack. Let's further suppose that he's entirely engaged by his work, having no concern for how it will be received or even whether it will be received in the outside world. To be sure, he wants to be a great painter; but he is not concerned about whether or not he will ever be considered one. Our Gauguin therefore possesses the subjective side of a meaningful life. It might seem here that we have someone who exhibits steadfastness and probably intensity in a trajectory that, while morally compromised, might not be said to be entirely immoral. Suppose, for instance, that this Gauguin's family is independently wealthy, and that his wife soon finds another suitor. Gauguin's life, as we imagine it, seems to have met the criteria of a meaningful life, both subjective and objectively. But would we want to call the life of Gauguin the hack a meaningful one?

In assessing this case, we should first distinguish it from another one. Our imagined Gauguin went to Tahiti to paint, not to play tiddlywinks or watch sports. This matters, because tiddlywinks and sports watching would not support the kinds of narrative values that painting does. As we saw above, certain kinds of activities or projects support certain kinds of narrative values, and some kinds of activities don't seem to support any narrative values at all. Gauguin chose a life project that supports particular narrative values. So the first question is whether he actually displayed those values. Did he commit to painting as doggedly as he could? Did he study colors, investigate light, learn drawing as best he could, think about settings and juxtaposition, practice his craft? If not, his life would seem to lack meaningfulness simply because he did not really exhibit the narrative values at issue.

But suppose he did all that. Suppose that the one thing standing between Gauguin and success was native talent. He did everything he could to succeed, but just didn't have the eye-hand coordination to pull it off. What do we say then?

It seems to me that we can clearly say that his life was meaningful. There is no disparity between meeting the criteria for meaningfulness I have laid out and our intuitions about whether our imagined Gauguin's life was meaningful. The two don't come apart. Here was a man, absorbed by what he did, and who displayed the dedication to his craft that might have made more talented painters successful. Why should we not call this life a meaningful one? Why should we make the meaningfulness of his life hinge on the luck of his having a particular skill?

To see this point, imagine things slightly differently. Suppose that our Gauguin did in fact have talent. He made great art. However, nobody ever saw it. He was never discovered, and his art died with him. Since he was interested in making art rather than being recognized, his obscurity did not bother him. For him, as for our previous Gauguin, it was not about fame; it was about the art. Would we have any reason to call our reimagined Gauguin a failure? It seems not. He led a life of commitment to his art, displayed both steadfastness and intensity, and was happy in the very way Haybron describes. Why should public recognition have any relevance in assessing the meaningfulness of his life?

The difference between our reimagined Gauguin and the previous one is talent. The new Gauguin is actually a good artist, where our original one was not. But if von Stauffenberg's life was meaningful even in its failure, and if lives that are never recognized can be meaningful, then there seems no bar to saying that our original Gauguin's life was indeed a meaningful one. The key here is that meaningfulness lies not in what is achieved or recognized, but in *how* a life is lived. Narrative values show us that the way we go about crafting our lives, whether consciously so or not, can determine their meaningfulness. This has nothing to do with success, no matter how much importance our world seems to accord to it.

To be sure, we cannot go so far as to say that luck plays *no* role in determining the meaningfulness of a life. A person dedicated to a life of athletics who suffers an injury that destroys his ability to compete will be unable to express certain narrative values. And if that dedication is central to his life, its meaningfulness may well be diminished. Had the Compsons all died young, or had Jimi Hendrix's fingers been mauled in an accident, the meaningfulness expressed in Dilsey's and Hendrix's lives would have been compromised. If luck played no part in determining the meaningfulness of a life, then we would have to allow that a meaningful life can be lived under any conditions, no matter how dire. And that seems to place too great a responsibility for meaningfulness on people whose situation allows them few options for narrative expression. We should instead recognize that, rather than laying the entire burden of meaningfulness on individuals whose circumstances are constricted or impoverished, it should be the moral task of the rest of us to contribute to removing or alleviating those circumstances.

I do not want to say, then, that meaningfulness is entirely divorced from fortune. But we should recognize that meaningfulness need not be held hostage to success. And this, in our world, is a source of hope for all of us who feel uncomfortable with the cult of accomplishment—and, in fact, socially recognized accomplishment—as the determinant of a worthwhile life.

Having gone this far, however, should we not go one step further? If it is not necessary for one to be successful in order for one's life to be meaningful, is it necessary for a life to be meaningful at all? Is there some obligation to live a meaningful life? Have people whose lives are not meaningful (or, more accurately, not very meaningful) according to the criteria I have described failed in some duty to themselves or to others?

They have not. Here is another place where meaningfulness and morality come apart. We all have obligations, to one extent or another, to live morally decent lives. This is why evil lives cannot be accounted as worth living at all and therefore are meaningless even when they express narrative values.

We are accountable to others in regard to how we treat them. But we are not accountable to them as to whether are lives are meaningful. We do not owe it to others or to ourselves to live meaningfully. If someone were to say, in the face of what I have described here as the character of a meaningful life, "Not interested," I would have no complaint against him. I would have no argument to put forward as to why he should, even if not interested, feel obliged to express some narrative value or another. Here, as before, meaningfulness is a bit like beauty. Nobody is obliged to create beauty, although we admire it when it appears. Similarly, no one has a duty to live meaningfully, but we often appreciate it when we come across such lives. To judge a life as meaningless, or relatively meaningless, is not to assess it as worthless. As we saw in chapter 4, meaningfulness is not the same thing as moral worthiness. One's value as a person is not raised or diminished by the degree to which one's life is meaningful.

The goal in asking about meaningfulness is not to know what a person is worth. It is to answer the questions we raised at the outset: Have we lived as we ought, or as we might? Have our lives been not just good but meaningful? Was there a point to them, or will there be? Or will we instead lie on our deathbed and say to ourselves, "It was the wrong life. I should have lived differently"? The point of reflecting on meaning is to confront the trajectory of our lives with the question of their significance. And to do so without the comfort of cosmic support.

There is a cost to such a confrontation. Camus accounted the cost of finding no answer. I have argued here that, his concerns aside, we can indeed find one. There is human meaning to be had in our silent universe. It is not the meaning that he sought, but it has a significance nevertheless. Narrative values provide a way of recognizing how the arc of our lives may (or may not) express something that might redeem them in our own eyes, make them seem to burn more brightly than Camus thought them capable.

The costs of endorsing narrative values, indeed the costs of endorsing any values, is that our lives might not live up to them. If narrative values are the standard, or at least one standard, of judging the meaningfulness of a life, it is possible that one's life will turn out to be meaningless, or at least relatively so. And while this does not mean that that life has no worth at all, for a life to lack meaning is, for many, to be bereft in a particularly painful way. For most of us, to feel that we have lived in a less than meaningful way would be a source of deep regret. It would seem like a waste of the precious few hours we have to spend upon this planet.

The other side of that coin, however, is that to have a standard of meaningfulness is to possess a tool that allows us to reflect upon our lives in a fruitful way. That tool invites us to ask whether a feeling of emptiness is characteristic only of the moment or of something larger. And if the latter, to have a sense of what might be done to address it. Narrative values don't tell us how to live our lives. They do not comprise a how-to manual. Instead they offer a framework for asking what the trajectory of our lives has amounted to, what meaning it has or has not expressed.

This is not everything. The realm of narrative values does not make the silent universe speak. But it is not nothing either. It is instead, for those of us who lie awake at night and wonder what we might amount to, a way of placing some answers a little closer to our grasp.

ACKNOWLEDGMENTS

There are many people with whom I have discussed various ideas in this book over the years, too many to thank individually. Please accept my appreciation collectively. The book itself started as a paper I gave at my home institution of Clemson University as well as at the University of Richmond and the New School for Social Research. In all of these places there was helpful discussion. As the conception of the manuscript developed, I received valuable guidance from Chris Grau, Mark Lance, Jeff McMahan, Ladelle McWhorter, and my wife Kathleen. Elizabeth Branch Dyson and Carol Fisher Saller shepherded the manuscript through the evaluation and production process deftly. This book is dedicated to Kathleen, David, Rachel, and Joel, for all of whom I wish a richness of narrative value.

NOTES

1. Albert Camus, *The Myth of Sisyphus*, in Gordon Marino, ed. *Basic Writings of Existentialism* (New York: Modern Library, 2004), 448.

2. Aristotle, *Nicomachean Ethics*, 1098a17–18.

3. Ibid., 1144a4–5.

4. Ethan Bronner, "College Students Aiming for High Marks in Income," *New York Times*, January 12, 1998, http://query.nytimes.com/gst/full page.html?res-9901E3DE1539F931A25752C0A96E958260&scp=2&sq=col lege%20students%20%22meaningful%20philosophy%20of%20life%22& st=cse, accessed March 13, 2014.

5. This argument goes back to Socrates' discussion with Euthyphro in Plato's dialogue *Euthyphro*. Socrates asks, "Is what is holy holy because the gods approve it, or do they approve it because it is holy?" As he gradually leads Euthyphro to admit, it must be the latter. What is holy must be distinct from the love the gods have for it, and therefore it cannot be reduced to the mere fact that the gods love it, just as what is carried must be distinct from the act of carrying it and what is led must be distinct from what leads it. If the holy exists, it cannot be the product of their love. It must instead be the object of it. "And so it is because it is holy that it is loved; it is not holy because it is loved." The holy, whatever it is, must be what it is that the gods love. It cannot arise from the love itself.

6. The World Database of Happiness can be found at: http://www1 .eur.nl/fsw/happiness/, accessed March 14, 2014; the *Journal of Happiness Studies* is at http://www.springer.com/social+sciences/well-being/jour nal/10902, accessed March 14, 2014; the *World Happiness Report* can be found at http://www.earth.columbia.edu/sitefiles/file/Sachs%20Writing /2012/World%20Happiness%20Report.pdf, accessed March 14, 2014; while the survey of happiness by countries is at http://247wallst.com

/2012/05/22/the-happiest-countries-in-the-world-2/3/, accessed March 14, 2014.

7. There is a plethora of recent writings on happiness. Among the most influential books are Daniel Gilbert's *Stumbling on Happiness* (New York: Knopf, 2006), Daniel Kahneman's *Thinking Fast and Slow* (New York: Farrar, Straus, and Giroux, 2011), and Richard Layard's *Happiness: Lessons from a New Science* (New York: Penguin, 2005). Ed Diener, sometimes known as "Dr. Happiness," has written numerous articles on the subject, and Martin Seligman was a founder of what has come to be called Positive Psychology.

8. John Stuart Mill, *Utilitarianism* (Indianapolis: Hackett Publishing, 1979), 8.

9. Ibid., 10.

10. Robert Nozick, *Anarchy, State, and Utopia* (New York: Basic Books, 1974), 42–45.

11. Daniel Haybron, *The Pursuit of Unhappiness: The Elusive Psychology of Well-Being* (Oxford: Oxford University Press, 2008), 111.

12. See, e.g., Mihaly Csikszentmihalyi, *Flow: The Psychology of Optimal Experience* (New York: Harper and Row, 1990).

13. Haybron, *The Pursuit of Unhappiness*, 147.

14. Ibid., 268.

15. Susan Wolf, *Meaning in Life and Why It Matters* (Princeton: Princeton University Press, 2010), 9.

16. Ibid., 9–10.

17. Ibid., 111.

18. Haybron himself recognizes this. He argues that happiness is only one—although very important—element of well-being, and that well-being is only the subjective side of what makes a human life good.

19. Wolf, *Meaning in Life*, 16.

20. Ibid., 28.

21. Ibid., 39.

22. Aristotle, *Nicomachean Ethics*, 1100b15–1101a20.

23. For some recent work on conceiving ourselves narratively, see Alasdair MacIntyre, *After Virtue* (London: Duckworth, 1981); Paul Ricoeur, *Oneself as Another*, trans. Kathleen Blamey (1990; repr. Chicago: University of Chicago Press, 1992); Adriana Cavarero, *Relating Narratives: Storytelling and Selfhood*, trans. Paul A. Kottman (1997; repr. London: Routledge, 2000);

Marya Schechtman, *The Constitution of Selves* (Ithaca: Cornell University Press, 1996).

24. Jerome Bruner, *Making Stories: Law, Literature, Life* (New York: Farrar, Strauss and Giroux, 2002), 85–86.

25. Galen Strawson, "Against Narrativity," *Ratio* 17, no. 4 (2004): 430.

26. Ibid., 433.

27. Strawson distinguishes what he calls a "form-finding tendency" from storytelling per se. For him, form-finding involves "some sort of relatively large-scale coherence-seeking, unity-seeking, pattern-seeking" (441) or equivalent. Storytelling, by contrast, involves actual narratives of some sort or another. Strawson's claim is that, "granted that certain sorts of self-understanding are necessary for a good human life, they need involve nothing more than form-finding, which can exist in the absence of Narrativity; and they may be osmotic, systemic, not staged in consciousness" (448).

28. Michel Foucault, "On the Genealogy of Ethics: An Overview of Work in Progress," in *The Foucault Reader*, ed. Paul Rabinow (1984; repr. Middlesex: Penguin, 1991), 350.

29. Italo Calvino, *Invisible Cities*, trans. William Weaver (New York: Harcourt Brace Jovanovich, 1974), 90–91.

30. Herman Melville, *Moby-Dick* (1851; repr. New York: Penguin 1972), 96.

31. For a good discussion of the various philosophical positions on love, as well as an interesting and original take on the issue, see Troy Jollimore's recent book *Love's Vision* (Princeton: Princeton University Press, 2011).

32. Wolf, *Meaning in Life*, 77.

33. Ibid., 78.

34. Aristotle, *Nicomachean Ethics*, 1094b25.

35. There are in the philosophy of science a number of debates about the ways in which theory orients how the world appears to an observer. For some, theory plays such an important role that they believe scientific theory is hardly constrained by the world. This would make the difficulties science faces with regard to objectivity much like those that values face.

36. Michel Foucault, *Discipline and Punish: The Birth of the Prison*, trans. Alan Sheridan (1975; repr. New York: Random House, 1977), 191.

37. Wilfrid Sellars, "Empiricism and the Philosophy of Mind," in *Minnesota Studies in the Philosophy of Science*, ed. Herbert Feigl and Michael

Scriven, vol. 1, *The Foundations of Science and the Concepts of Psychology and Psychoanalysis* (Minneapolis: University of Minnesota Press, 1956), sec. 38.

38. In particular, the philosopher Robert Brandom, from whom I learned about Sellars, and Mark Lance, a student of Brandom's who helped me navigate through the thickets of Sellars's and Brandom's philosophies as well as developing his own view of these matters.

39. I offer my own solution in a book I published some years ago, *Our Practices, Our Selves* (University Park: Penn State Press, 2000).

40. Bernard Williams, "Moral Luck," in *Moral Luck: Philosophical Papers, 1973–1980* (Cambridge: Cambridge University Press, 1981). The description of this particular Gauguin is on 22–23.

SUGGESTIONS FOR
FURTHER READING

The philosophical literature on what makes life meaningful is not as extensive as one might hope. It is an important concern in ancient philosophy, although, as our discussion of Aristotle indicates, it is framed differently from the way we think of it now. In the twentieth century, Camus, Sartre, and the existentialists brought it to the fore. More recently, Susan Wolf's *Meaning in Life and Why It Matters*, which inspired this work, is causing conversation in the philosophical world.

A good overview of philosophical discussion on the meaning of life, recently updated, is Thaddeus Metz's entry "The Meaning of Life" in the online Stanford Encyclopedia of Philosophy (http://plato.stanford.edu/entries/life-meaning/). (The Stanford Encyclopedia of Philosophy is a good philosophical source for just about anything.) And an excellent collection of articles is E. D. Klemke and Steven M. Cahn's *The Meaning of Life: A Reader* (New York: Oxford University Press, 2008). As far as specific positions go, Antti Kauppinen's "Meaningfulness and Time" (in *Philosophy and Phenomenological Research* 84, no. 2 (March 2012): 345–77) takes Wolf's approach and develops a view of what makes life meaningful that takes into account the trajectory of life. In this way, his work and mine start from the same place and have similar motivations. Kauppinen's approach, however, is very different from the one in this book. I find it fascinating, but to my mind a bit narrow, partly due to the Aristotelean character of his view. Another narratively inflected take on what makes life meaningful is John Martin Fischer's "Stories and the Meaning of Life," from his book *Our Stories: Essays on Life, Death, and Free Will* (Oxford: Oxford University Press, 2009), 165–77. Fischer relates meaningfulness to creativity and free will. An important earlier source of Kauppinen's, Fischer's, and my own approach is J. David Velleman's article "Well-Being and Time," from *Pacific Philosophical Quarterly* 72 (1991): 48–77. Velleman discusses well-being rather than meaningfulness, but approaches it in a narrative fashion. An earlier, more straightforwardly Aristotelean approach is Alasdair MacIntyre's *After Virtue* (South Bend: Notre Dame University Press, 1981).

One more discussion is worth mentioning. Richard Taylor's book *Good and Evil: A New Direction* (London: Macmillan, 1970) has a concluding chapter arguing for a subjective view of the meaningfulness of life. (He also has a later article with a different view, "Time and Life's Meaning," which argues that it is creativity that makes life meaningful, and that creativity is a rare phenomenon. That article appears in *Review of Metaphysics* 40 (June 1987): 675–86. The subjective view is challenged by a difficult but very influential article by David Wiggins, "Truth, Invention and the Meaning of Life," which appears in his book *Needs, Values, Truth: Essays in the Philosophy of Value*, 2nd ed. (Oxford: Basil Blackwell, 1991). Wiggins defends a more nearly objectivist view, but one that does not seek to rely on God or some other transcendent foundation.

As far as happiness goes, I offer a few references in notes 6 and 7 of the introduction. The literature on happiness, and the related concept of well-being, is vast and, as the text argues, a distinct area from that of meaningfulness. The Stanford Encyclopedia of Philosophy also offers an excellent summary of the field from a philosophical perspective with Daniel Haybron's entry (http://plato.stanford.edu/entries/happiness/).

INDEX

Haybron, Daniel (*continued*) 94–95, 109, 115, 177, 181; on psychic affirmation, 45–48
Hendrix, Jimi, 75, 79, 81–83, 91–92, 98–99, 110, 118, 136, 182
Hepburn, Katherine, 119
Hitchens, Christopher, 14

James, Henry, 105, 108, 134; *Portrait of a Lady*, 105–116, 121
James, William, 105
Johnson, Lyndon, 77
Joplin, Janis, 75
Jordan, Michael, 119
Joyce, James, 37

King, Jr., Martin Luther, 77
Kuhn, Thomas, 3

literature: and narrative values, 134–136
love, 94–96

Melville, Herman, 93
Mengele, Joseph, 129
Michelangelo, 12
Mill, John Stuart, 40–42, 45
morality: and limits of meaningfulness, 124–129; without meaningfulness, 110–116; meaningfulness without morality, 117–124
music: and narrative values, 132–134

narrative therapy, 65–66
narrative values: adventurousness, 76, 87, 93–94; contrasted with aesthetic values, 130–138; contrasted with moral values, 103, 110, 136–137, 159–160, 182–183; courage, 76, 79, 127; creativity, 76; definition, 73; gracefulness, 76; intellectual curiosity, 76; intensity, 23, 75–76, 88–92, 120–121, 134–135, 166; personal integrity, 76; spirituality, 76, 78–79, 82, 84; spontaneity, 23, 76, 81; steadfastness, 23, 72–73, 77–78, 97, 100, 106–112, 162–163; subtlety, 23, 76, 80–81, 92–93, 164–165
narrativity, 63–71
New York Times, 8
Nozick, Robert, 43

painting: and narrative values, 130–132
Parker, Dorothy, 119
Pol Pot, 125
Ptolemy, 140–141

relativism of values, 167–169
Rothko, Mark, 130–131

Sellars, Wilfrid, 156–158, 171
Shakespeare, ix
soccer, 144–147, 152–153, 159–161
Strawson, Galen, 67–69, 71, 73, 84, 85–86
success: contrasted with meaningfulness, 177–182

Tolstoy, Leo, 18

Van Gogh, Vincent, 130–132
von Stauffenberg, Claus, 114–116, 179, 181

White, Michael, 65
Williams, Bernard, 179

Winfrey, Oprah, 106, 108
Wittgenstein, Ludwig, 172
Wolf, Susan, 50–59, 76, 89, 102, 111, 114; definition of meaningfulness, 51; objective meaningfulness, 53–59